MENTORING

How to Invest Your Life in Others

By Tim Elmore

FOREWORD BY JOHN MAXWELL

Ministries Committed to Mentoring and Leadership

 EQUIP, a not-for-profit Christian organization, is devoted to the singular purpose of developing Christ-like leaders in the most influential and neglected parts of our world. Believing that everything rises and falls on leadership, EQUIP is strategically investing in the lives of leaders in: the *international arena*; the *academic arena* and the *urban arena*. This ministry is also enlisting one million people to pray for their pastor. EQUIP lives out it's mission through conducting leadership conferences, producing leadership curriculum and providing leadership mentoring opportunities.

EQUIP: 1-888-993-7847

 Emerging Young Leaders (EYL) is a nonprofit organization dedicated to training and mentoring the world's emerging young leaders for significant service and the development of others. They are using both mentoring and training experiences to develop leaders in the home, academic, business and church settings. EYL is recruiting spiritually mature mentors around the world to invest themselves in high school and college-age mentees, as well conducting mentor-training workshops and developing mentoring resources.

EYL: 1-888-395-6687

KBM

Kingdom Building Ministries is a ministry committed to raising up a new generation of "laborers" for Kingdom service worldwide. They are mobilizing the Church to get out of the "pew" and into the "harvest field". The primary tools KBM offers are itinerant speakers and mentoring resources, designed for both churches and colleges. KBM desires to partner with local churches to mentor people that will incarnate Kingdom values, and join in the cause of the Great Commission.

KBM: 1-800-873-8957

CONTENTS

   This chapter provides definition to mentoring and how it
   looks in everyday life. It reveals different styles of
   mentoring and how to approach it as a ministry.

   This chapter communicates the necessity of life on life
   investment, and how intimacy, accountability and real
   impact can only be achieved in smaller clusters.

   Women possess certain qualities that enable them to
   mentor effectively. They also face specific temptations that
   they must avoid. This chapter identifies the strengths we
   must emulate, the cautions we must heed, and provides
   practical tips to improve mentoring skills.

   Men approach mentoring differently than women. This
   chapter highlights their strengths, then communicates why
   relationships are difficult for the male gender. It closes with
   a list of practical steps men can take to become more
   effective communicators.

This chapter will guide a point person on how to set up structures for mentoring in their church from a grass roots level. It only takes one person who will take the right steps.

This final chapter communicates exactly how a mentor can make the most of their time with a mentee. Instruction is given on how to form questions, probe hearts and sustain accountability.

FOREWORD

I have been interested in leadership my entire adult life. During my twenty-seven years as a pastor, I taught leadership not only to my staff, but to tens of thousands of other pastors across the country.

One of the conclusions I've drawn is that the art of mentoring is all about fleshing out the functions of a leader, in a single relationship. This handbook on mentoring will be a literal guide to you, as you seek to lead people, one life at a time. Tim Elmore and I have had hours of conversation and application on this issue, and we both believe that mentoring is the first and last task of a leader. It is the first task of a leader because everyone who wants to lead the "masses" ought to begin by leading one person. It is the last or ultimate task of a leader because the acid test of any leader is—are they able to reproduce themselves in others? Success without a successor is a failure. Both leadership and mentoring are about spiritual multiplication. Both are about developing people.

I love Tim Elmore. He and I have been in a mentoring relationship ourselves, for the last fourteen years. He is now communicating the principles that he lived and practiced as a pastor in San Diego—to thousands of pastors and lay leaders around the world. I can promise you that you will be enriched with every chapter you read from this comprehensive manual. It will act as a sort of "mentor" to you on how to mentor others. May you go on to add value to others as you develop them, and multiply yourself in them.

Dr. John Maxwell
Founder, Injoy / EQUIP

How to get the most out of this book!
(An Introduction)

Some would say that mentoring is just a fad, just a buzzword that happens to be popular in our generation and within our culture.

I disagree. I am obviously elated about the current trend toward mentors connecting with proteges. But I believe it is much more than a trend. The fact of the matter is, every great movement of God in history has been sustained through two vehicles: (1) the truths and distinctives of that movement were committed to paper, and (2) the initial leaders mentored a second generation of leaders. John Wesley, for example, employed both of these vehicles as the great Methodist movement took root over two hundred years ago. He was committed to mentoring young preachers and setting up "class meetings" (accountability groups) to nurture spiritual growth in his followers. I still remember visiting Epworth and Bristol in England and seeing the results of Wesley's mentoring ministry. He built a chapel in Bristol where he could watch (from a glass window above the sanctuary) his young, emerging ministers as they preached. Later, he would meet with them and evaluate their progress. It is my belief that this is what gave permanence to his movement as opposed to George Whitefield's, a contemporary of Wesley. George Whitefield was a more sought after public orator and drew the largest crowds of any preacher in his generation. John Wesley, however, was committed to spiritual reproduction; he determined to mentor young men.

The purpose of this handbook is simple. I am *not* attempting to replace the magnificent books that have already been written on the subject of mentoring. As you turn the page in a moment, you will see I have cited some of the best books on mentoring from our own generation. These books are "must reading" as far as I'm concerned.

What I am attempting to do, however, is provide a practical and speedy reference book, to be referred to over and over again, as you engage in the practice of mentoring. There is not a large amount of philosophy to wade through here. Instead, there are handy insights and easy-to-use lists to implement that have been tested and proven over time. I have laid out the material in a "question and answer" format, drawing from the most qualified experts in the field as well as my own experience and observation. This is literally a bottom-line reference book on the subject. In fact, I will suggest four different ways this book could be useful to you:

1. Read it through for your own personal enrichment.
2. Use it as a source to train others in the art of mentoring.
3. Study and discuss it in a small group setting.
4. Utilize it as a reference guide as you encounter questions.

My goal is to provide practical "handles" to theoretical truth. I want to mentor you in the art of mentoring.

Here is my conviction for doing so. I believe we cannot accomplish the work of God, en masse. We have all seen the big "programs" in our local churches where we've attempted to "disciple" people in "assembly-line" fashion, cranking out committed and intimate followers of Jesus from a classroom or sanctuary setting. I don't believe that's the most effective method for producing disciples or laborers. (Otherwise, every church in America would have plenty of disciples and laborers!) While I do believe there is a place for the classroom and corporate worship/body life, true disciples or laborers are best developed through life-on-life mentoring. It requires making deposits in people, one life at a time. It's what Jesus did with the twelve.

That is what this handbook calls you to be and do. It is difficult. It is slow. It often seems like poor stewardship of your time. But with the right individuals, the payoffs are extraordinary. Like Jesus, I am speaking of a "movement" not a program. Programs usually start big...and then, as their novelty wanes, they fizzle and become small. Movements, on the other hand, generally start very small...and become huge! Let's begin the adventure now!

Resources

This handbook is a synthesis of both personal experience and the reading of timely books on the subject. Many of the practical insights you'll find here are the result of the work of men far wiser than I. I acknowledge their contribution and recommend these resources to you for further study:

- Chris Adsit   *Personal Disciplemaking*/ Thomas Nelson Publishers/1988

- Bobb Biehl   *Mentoring*/Broadman & Holman/1996

- Dr. Robert Clinton   *Connecting*/Navpress/1992
  & Paul Stanley

     The Mentor Handbook/ Barnabas Publishers/1990

- Dr. Robert Coleman   *The Master Plan of Evangelism*/ F. Revell/1963

- Dr. Ted Engstrom   *The Fine Art of Mentoring*/ Wolgemuth & Hyatt Publishers, Inc./1989

- Dr. Howard Hendricks   *As Iron Sharpens Iron*/ Moody Press/1995

- Bill Hull   *The Disciple Making Pastor*/ F. Revell/1988

• Dr. John Maxwell

Developing The Leader Within You/Thomas Nelson Publishers/1993

Developing The Leaders Around You/Thomas Nelson Publishers/1995

• David Rosage

Beginning Spiritual Direction/Servant Publications/1994

"PLEASE
MENTOR ME"

An Open Letter From "Generation X"

It is an image indelibly etched into the American conscious-
ness: four of the fastest men in the world poised at the start
of the 4 x 100 relay at the 1988 Olympics. Comprised of a
peerless group of athletes, each a champion in his own right,
it was inconceivable that the United States team could lose.
Yet as the final leg of the race approached, the unthinkable
happened. The Americans dropped the baton. Quick as light-
ening it was over. The race and any hopes of a gold medal were
lost. The crowd, electrified moments earlier, was struck mute.
All the potential nullified because of a botched hand-off.

For many of us who fall in the age group known as the "Baby
Busters" or "Generation X" (born between 1965 and 1983), this
disastrous scene aptly describes the sense of loss we feel entering adulthood. Searching desperately for godly mentors to teach
us, yet not knowing where to look, we are left feeling like runners
stranded at the starting gate without a baton. Some may charac-
terize us as lazy "slackers," but the truth is. . .ours is a traumatized
generation lacking direction and identity, missing a sense of con-
tinuity with our heritage. It underscores our need for mature,
older men to come alongside us, to share their wisdom, and hand
us the torch of leadership to equip the next generation.

In the Old Testament we find that a young man, to be considered a true Jew, was required to trace his lineage to Abraham.
Yet many of us in the 90s scarcely know our own fathers. We

are so many "Timothys" looking for "Pauls" to link us with our past and steer us into the future. While we may appear aloof or even distrustful, it is because we have been disappointed so often. We hunger for your friendship. We thirst after your godly character. We ask ourselves: "Where are the men to accept us with no strings attached, to let us serve alongside them without fear of failure? Where are the men willing to share their mistakes so that we might not repeat them? Where are the men willing to love us enough not to leave us the way we are?"

Will you take a risk with us, and allow us to serve alongside you in the spiritual warfare we all face? Will you let us share with you our burning passion for Jesus Christ while receiving the treasure of your experience? Bridging the gap is not as hard as you might think...all we're really asking is for a chance to make a new beginning, so together we might work to raise the standard of this world. History tells us that no revival has ever spanned two consecutive generations. Perhaps ours is the generation for the next century. We need you to help us find our place in a confusing world. Please don't leave us standing at the starting gate.

Signed,
Looking for mentors

(This letter appeared in a 1995 newsletter sent out by "Promise Keepers.")

WHAT IS MENTORING?

I have to admit, I was a little proud. My good friend Rob had just won the award for being "Teacher of the Year" at the high school where he taught. I had the privilege of attending the banquet that would honor him.

At the close of the evening, he was asked to make a speech disclosing what his "secret" was to impacting students. Everyone seemed to wonder what made him unique. Just how had he made such a difference in their lives? Rob stood poised at the small oak podium, prepared to answer these profound questions. He cleared his throat and began to speak. He told stories of students who had made right choices about their lives and literally engineered a turn-around for the good. As he concluded, he attempted to summarize his part in the process: "I guess my secret was that I made the move from merely being a *teacher* to being a *mentor* to these teens."

Indeed, he had. I had personally watched him all year making priceless investments into the lives of those young people. And tonight, Rob was saying a mouthful. He had become a mentor to so many of them. There was a strange quietness in the room that night. Although no one said it out loud, I am certain that the majority of the audience didn't get it. I think they were filled with unspoken confusion: What's the big secret? What's the difference between a teacher and a mentor?

The truth is, there is often a marked difference in our Western society. While every mentor is, indeed, a teacher—not every teacher is a mentor.

COMING TO TERMS

No doubt, the term "mentoring" has become a popular "buzzword." Unfortunately, it has accumulated various definitions on its road to fame. At Rob's award banquet, there likely were dozens of images that raced across the minds of his audience when he used the word. We all seem to be on different pages.

It will serve us well, then, to offer a working definition at the beginning of this handbook. Developed by Paul Stanley and Robert Clinton, it reads as follows:

> *Mentoring is a relational experience*
> *through which one person empowers another*
> *by sharing God-given resources.*

The resources vary. Mentoring is a positive dynamic that enables people to develop potential.

Since the rash of leadership failures between 1985 and 1995, more people recognize the need for accountability in leadership. Adequate mentoring might have prevented most of these failures. Certainly the kind of mentoring described in this handbook can help prevent failures in leadership and give that needed accountability. Leaders want to finish well. They would welcome mentoring if they saw it as an enhancement to their growth.

Mentoring can reduce the probability of leadership failure, provide needed accountability, and empower a responsive, potential laborer. John C. Crosby of The Uncommon Individual Foundation writes, "mentoring is a brain to pick, a shoulder to cry on, and a kick in the seat of the pants."

In their book *Connecting*, Stanley and Clinton continue with this helpful perspective. Usually when people are first introduced to mentoring, they think of an ideal mentor—a perfect model who can do almost everything. Few of those exist. The myth about mentoring is that it requires some hyper-gifted guru, just dripping with God's anointing. In this handbook we want to put mentoring in the practical realm: Anyone can mentor, provided he has learned something from God and is willing to share with others what he has learned.

I remember my first attempts at mentoring. I was filled with the usual sense of inadequacy as I considered what I would say to someone that could actually change their life. I finally had to scrap my original stereotypes of white haired, all-wise mentors and simply begin a relationship with someone that I felt I was a step or two ahead of in my spiritual journey. I ended up choosing seven high school students. We met together each week for a structured meeting and then enjoyed several informal experiences that bonded us relationally. Five of those seven students are now in full-time ministry. Soon I was mentoring interns at the church where I worked. What a joy it is today to see them pastoring churches, counseling, working as missionaries, teaching, planting churches and ministering in parachurch organizations. I feel like a proud parent!

As a follower of Christ, you can mentor others. Whatever God has given you that has enabled you to grow and deepen your relationship with Him, you can pass on to others. For example, introducing young followers of Christ to the basics of spiritual growth (the process of discipleship) is the first and most basic type of mentoring. You need to know that there are various styles of mentoring, too. According to my research, there are more than a half a dozen different kinds of mentors that can play a role in someone's life. We must stop stereotyping. In Chapter 7, I outline these different kinds of mentors, noting that we all need a variety of them based on the stage of life we are experiencing. In addition, we will naturally flourish serving as a certain kind of mentor (to someone else) based on the person God has created us to be.

Reading about the heroes of the past, or historical models, is another form of mentoring that can happen anytime. Observing the growth, struggles, responses, and decision-making processes of those who have lived before can provide insight, challenge, and often practical help for our own situations.

Consider this. Occasionally, God may bring a person into your life who makes a timely contribution: a word of counsel, an insight, a question or encouragement. These "divine contacts" will not usually know how they are being used in your life, but you can take advantage of them as God-given resources sent along at the right moment. They are, in fact, a sort of mentor to you.

This will probably be true for you as well, as *you* assume the role of a mentor. There will be moments you will share a simple insight or truth (that you may have picked up years ago) and doing so, you will change the perspective of your mentee forever! There will be times you will "speak into their life" with authority and wisdom—and not realize how profound your words really are. Simply put, people mentoring people are God's method for making disciples!

MENTORING THROUGH THE YEARS

Interestingly, mentoring is not a new concept. For example, mentoring happened in some form in ancient Greek and Hebrew cultures. Both had their own "model" for making disciples. The Greek philosopher Socrates discipled Plato; Plato discipled Aristotle; Aristotle discipled Alexander the Great. Their disciple-making process, however, was different than that of the Hebrews in the Old and New Testament. It is the *Hebrew* model that I am advocating here in this book. Let me explain why.

While Americans have embraced the Greek model for learning, the Hebrew model has been employed by God's people for centuries, especially during the days of the Bible. The Greek model I have referred to is what I call the "classroom" model. This takes place when teachers assume their place up front, and students passively listen to a lecture. It is academic in nature; it is cerebral and cognitive. It is passive. And while it is the fastest method to transfer information to another person or group, it is not the most effective method for the student to learn. Learning happens much more efficiently through the Hebrew model, where the teacher or mentor invites the student to travel with them. No doubt, the mentor has much to say through verbal *instruction,* but this is not the only tool in their pocket. They *demonstrate* the principles they want their mentees to embrace in a real life context. Then they let those mentees try their hand at it themselves. They understand that the best way to learn is to *experience* something firsthand. Finally, they give time for debriefing and feedback. They provide *accountability* and assessment. In short, the following table summarizes the contrast between these two learning models:

GREEK MODEL	HEBREW MODEL
1. *The Classroom Model*	1. *The Coach Model*
2. Academic	2. Relational
3. Passive	3. Experiential
4. Theoretical	4. On the Job Training

These two learning methods received their titles from the culture in which they were popularized. Long before Jesus came along and chose twelve men to mentor, the ancient Greek culture was making disciples, as I've mentioned, with Socrates and Plato; Plato and Aristotle, etc. But the mentoring was much more philosophical in nature than with the Hebrew culture. It was more academic than relational. It was more passive than experiential. It was, in fact, much more like the classrooms of our schools and churches across the United States than what Jesus did for His disciples. For instance, it would have been common to ask a student from the Greek culture the question: "What subjects are you studying?" This would also be very common in our American colleges today. In the Hebrew culture, however, the question was not "what are you studying?" but rather, "who are you studying under?" The emphasis was on the *mentor,* not the *material.*

Jesus treated his disciples or mentees more like *apprentices*, than academicians. Theirs was "on-the-job training." You can imagine how that must have accelerated their learning curve! Can you visualize how much more quickly Simon Peter must have grasped how Jesus cast out demons when he knew Jesus was going to ask him to do it the following Thursday? The fact of the matter is, this is what "mentoring" is all about. It is recognizing that humans "own" truth much more quickly when it is learned from relationship and experience than from a sterile classroom.

THE EVOLUTION OF EDUCATION

Mentoring is as old as civilization itself. Through this natural relational process, experience and values pass from one generation to another. Mentoring took place among Old Testament prophets (Eli and Samuel, Elijah and Elisha) and leaders (Moses and Joshua), and New Testament leaders (Barnabas and Paul, Paul and Timothy). Throughout human history, mentoring was the primary means of passing on knowledge and skills in every field—from Greek philosophers to sailors—and in every culture. But in the modern age, the learning process shifted. It now relies primarily on computers, classrooms, books, and videos. Thus, the relational connection between the knowledge-and-experience giver and the receiver has weakened or is nonexistent.

Society is now rediscovering that the process of learning and maturing needs time and many kinds of relationships. The "self-made" man or woman is a myth and, though some claim it, few aspire to it. It leaves people relationally deficient and narrow-minded. The resurgence of mentoring in virtually every occupational field and area of life is a response to this discovery. "Please mentor me," is the spoken and unspoken request expressed by so many today.

A BIBLICAL EXAMPLE

Barnabas was a people influencer. He saw potential in Saul (later the Apostle Paul) when others kept their distance. Saul's conversion turned this brilliant zealot of orthodox Judaism into a fearless Christian evangelist, an apologist. Both Jews and the original disciples alike feared him and were afraid to let him join them. "But Barnabas took him [Saul] and brought him to the apostles" (Acts 9:27). Barnabas was not intimidated by this brash convert, but drew him in and vouched for him. Undoubtedly, he encouraged and taught Saul during those early days and patiently stayed with him, knowing that time and experience would soon temper and mature this gifted young leader.

Later, when the gospel spread to Antioch and "a great number of people believed and turned to the Lord" (Acts 11:21), the apostles sent Barnabas (the Encourager) to the city to verify the phenomenon as genuine. Seeing that the gospel had truly borne fruit and that God's grace was at work, Barnabas knew they would need teaching and growth. So he went to Tarsus to find Saul and bring him back to Antioch to help, as he was a powerful teacher and understood the Greek mind and culture. Barnabas (the mentor) knew the kind of developmental environment and challenge that Saul needed in order to grow, and drew him into it. Thank God for Barnabas and the gift he gave the Church by taking an interest in young Saul! How many Sauls are in the Church today just waiting for a Barnabas?

Interestingly, Barnabas did such a thorough job with Saul that Saul later took on mentees himself. Young men such as Titus, Timothy, Silas and even a couple, Aquila and Priscilla. He later became so convinced of the necessity of mentoring and spiritual reproduction that he wrote to his mentee: "And the things which you've received from me, entrust these to faithful men who will be able to teach others also." (2 Timothy 2:2)

Paul and Barnabas illustrate a number of the specific ways that mentors help mentees:

- Ability to readily see potential in a person
- Tolerance with mistakes, brashness, abrasiveness, and the like in order to see that potential develop
- Flexibility in responding to people and circumstances
- Patience, knowing that time and experience are needed for development
- Perspective, having vision and ability to see down the road and suggest the next steps that a mentee needs
- Gifts and abilities that build up and encourage others
- Timely words of counsel and insight
- Resources such as letters, articles, books, etc.

Kingdom Building Ministries, for instance, has seen the results of positive mentoring. Having received from those who've gone before them, the staff have committed themselves to the mentoring process. Diane was a school teacher who decided to take some time away from her classroom and be mentored at the Denver, Colorado institute (now called The Laborer's Institute). Following this experience, she determined God was calling her overseas as a single woman. She now ministers to students in China. Incidentally, she found her husband in the process of serving in China.

Dave was a student who already knew God was calling him to be a "laborer" full time. After his mentoring experience, he not only carved out a statement of purpose for his life, but now serves other students at a large church in California.

On the other coast, Ken returned to South Carolina to his law practice, after being mentored by some staff at KBM. He cut his work as an attorney to part time and enrolled in seminary. He's working toward combining ministry with his practice, and will probably impact thousands of lives before he's finished.

My point is not to say mentoring forces people into ministry, but simply that it has dramatic effects on the life decisions of the mentees.

THE BOTTOM LINE

These mentoring stories share some common features. They started with someone in need. This person met someone further along in experience who had something to contribute to that need. A relationship was established. The more experienced person shared what he had been through or learned, meeting the needs of the first person. With the acceptance of what was shared, the power to grow through a situation was passed from the mentor to the mentee. It was not just a sharing and receiving of information, actual change took place. We refer to this transfer between mentor and mentee as *empowerment*. This process is the heart of mentoring.

Mentoring is popular at present. It's popularity attests to its potential usefulness for leadership development. It also speaks of the tremendous relational vacuum in an individualistic society and its accompanying lack of accountability. In *Habits of the Heart*, the authors see individualism as an American asset turned into a liability. Americans cling to personal independence when they desperately need interdependence. God did not create people to be self-sufficient and move through life alone. To return to healthy relational living will require recognition of this need and courage to change. In no other area, is this change so urgently needed than in leadership development. Acknowledgment of this need is partially responsible for the groundswell toward mentoring. "Will you mentor me?" is being expressed in many ways in every area: business, ministry, family, military, education, and the church. This swelling cry for meaningful relationships can be a springboard to learning and growth via the art of mentoring.

I hope you sense something of the potential that mentoring may have for you in unleashing God's power in your life through special relationships with others. Perhaps you are beginning to sense that God may want you to establish relationships with others that will make a difference. May this be said of you, as you mentor others:

A MENTOR IS A PEOPLE GROWER

He has a sort of green thumb
When it comes to handling folks.
He'll listen to their troubles,
He'll chuckle at their jokes.
Somehow they know his interest
Is genuine and true,
And right before your eyes you'll see
Them grow an inch or two.
You'll see their faces blossom out
In smiles of budding cheer.
You know they've found a ray of hope
To drive away their fear;
You know he's sowed the seeds of faith
And showered them with love,
And made them sense the presence
Of the good Lord up above.
He clears out all the weeds of doubt
And fear and hate and greed
And gives them room to breathe. He seems
To sense their every need.
He nurtures them with praises for
The good things that they've done
and trains them to look upward
And to stand tall in the sun.
He has a sort of green thumb
Like a farmer with the sod —
But his work is growing people
In the image of his God.

Helen Lowerie Marshall

Probably the greatest word picture for what mentoring is all about can be summarized in the little story of a boy and his dad walking down a rocky road one evening. After stumbling and falling to the ground, the boy looked up at his father and said, "Dad, why don't you watch where I'm going?" I believe we can say with great accuracy that that is what mentoring is all about—watching where others are going.

FROM THE BEGINNING

Before you tread any further through this handbook, I'd like to ask you some questions. Please reflect on them prior to reading the next chapter. Consider these questions "friendly accountabilty." I want to ensure, as much as I can, that this book won't simply provide mental stimulation, but mentor application! Consider your answers to these questions:

QUESTIONS...

1. Do you have any truly intimate relationships/friendships? Who are those people?

2. Do you have people fulfilling the following roles for you:
   • A Paul (mentor): _____
   • A Barnabas (accountability partner): _____
   • A Timothy (a mentee): _____

3. Do you know one or two individuals that could benefit from your mentoring?

4. What would be the best way to approach them? When would be the best time?

WHY IS MENTORING NECESSARY?

Is mentoring really necessary? Wouldn't it be possible to pull off what God commands us to do without all the trouble it requires? Is it possible to impact the world and not bother with "one-to-one" ministry?

These are good questions. They are ones that the Church has knowingly or unknowingly been asking for hundreds of years. I say this because all but a remnant of the Body of Christ has refused to make such personal and painstaking investments down through the centuries. Beginning in 313 A.D., when Emperor Constantine declared Christianity the official religion of the Roman Empire, Christians have typically chosen the easy route. The Christian faith became institutionalized. Parishes began to rely on the paid clergy to do ministry. The making of disciples, through relationships, came grinding to a slow crawl. Eventually, Christianity came to be associated with stained glass, impersonal worship services and institutions.

It seems obvious that our refusal to engage in mentoring relationships and discipleship contributed to this paradigm. Further, I believe it contributed to leading the Church into the "Dark Ages." The mentoring that did occur was predominantly confined to monasteries and disassociated from society at large. Again, it was relegated to a remnant. Unfortunately, this left the Church in a pitiful state of ignorance and compromise. In contrast, as we watch Jesus relate to His twelve disciples, we see that mentoring was His method to raise up "laborers." (Matthew 9:37-10:8) He spent time investing in this small cluster of men—as much or more than He did in public ministry to the masses. This is why organizations like the EQUIP Foundation, Emerging Young Leaders and Kingdom Building Ministries have included the term "mentoring" in their list of "core values." KBM followed it with this descriptive phrase:

> Mentoring—Laborers cannot be mass produced, but are raised up through life on life mentoring.

Consider this truth: Leadership can be viewed on three levels. From least effective to most effective, these levels may be defined this way:

LEVEL ONE: IMPRESS
The leader impresses followers. This can be done with little or no relationship. It requires only the will of the leader to be involved. He must want to leave a memorable impression on the followers.

LEVEL TWO: INFLUENCE
The leader influences followers. This can be done with some relationship between the two. It requires the will of the follower to be involved. He must want to be influenced by the leader.

LEVEL THREE: IMPACT
The leader impacts followers. This can only be done through intimate relationship. It requires both the will of the leader and follower to be involved. They must agree to accountability and growth.

Notice that all three levels change the follower in some way, but life change dramatically increases as the conditions of level three are met. Level one can be done within the context of the masses; level two requires a bit more relationship and commitment; but level three can only occur when intimate covenant is agreed upon and practiced. Impact requires some form of mentoring.

At this point in my life, I have intentionally mentored almost two hundred people, either one to one or in a small group. I have failed as often as I have succeeded in being and doing exactly what my mentee needed at the moment. I have cringed and cried when I've thought about some of my earlier days in ministry— attempting to "pour my life" into someone, but not knowing just how to do it. Thank God for merciful mentees, who were happy to gain whatever they could from someone like me. As I reflect for a moment, however, I am convinced of at least one truth. No matter how poorly I played my role as mentor, those relationships were always better than if I'd only performed some massive ministry from a platform or pulpit. In other words, even my feeble attempts at mentoring are better than my best attempts at impressing someone from the stage. Good, honest attempts at developmental relationships are better than no attempts at all.

Dr. Robert Clinton has popularized an axiom that has directed the course of many successful ministries. It could be called the Principle of the Narrow Wedge. Read it over a couple of times. It goes like this: "More time with less people—equals greater impact for the Kingdom." Jesus demonstrated this principle time and time again with His disciples.

WHAT MAKES MENTORING UNIQUE?

Mentoring is unique from most church programs in that it is so focused. The surest way to secure your impact on people is to enter an accountable relationship with the conscious objective to produce measurable growth. This cannot be done with large groups. In fact, most small groups ministering in churches today don't mentor people well. Fellowship, love and nurture are all naturally fostered in them, but true mentoring is conspicuously absent.

So often we define mentoring in broad, all inclusive terms and miss what is really meant by the practice of developmental relationships and life-on-life investment.

For instance, while it is possible to inadvertently mentor someone in the course of normal church programming, it is rare. Mentoring usually does not happen effectively in a large worship service, a typical Sunday school class, or even an average small group. Consequently, as you consider mentoring people in a small group context, Sunday school class or group leadership training, please note the distinctives of a mentoring relationship below. The following is a table that contrasts what normally happens in a small group versus what happens in an effective mentoring relationship. While there is some overlap in the relational focus, note the differences that set mentoring apart from group ministry. My challenge to you is to become a true mentor to the people you serve.

Small Groups	**Mentoring**
1. Focus is on relationships and fellowship	1. Focus is on giving and receiving direction

2. Context is community	2. Context is personal
3. Discussion oriented	3. Application oriented
4. Normal size: ten to fifteen	4. Normal size: one on one to one on three
5. Value depends on the group	5. Value depends on the mentor
6. Content based on curriculum	6. Content based on need of mentee
7. Leader's goal is collective spiritual growth	7. Mentor's goal is intentional investment
8. Progress is often sporadic	8. Progress is made by predetermined goals
9. Success measured by health of group	9. Success measured by life change of one
10. Low level of accountability	10. High, intense level of accountability
11. Body life (heart and mind)	11. Discipleship (heart, will and mind)
12. Purpose is to meet together	12. Purpose is to reach potential

Consequently, the answer to the question, "Is mentoring really necessary?" can only be answered when we respond to a second question: How deeply do we want to impact people? I trust your answer to both questions will be reflections of Jesus and His methods.

HOW ARE WOMEN UNIQUE IN MENTORING?

In 1987 I took my first mission trip behind the iron curtain. I led a team of young adults from my church to minister in Budapest, Hungary. It was a marvelous experience for all of us. One of the greatest lessons I learned on that trip was the tremendous amount of labor that's involved in building a cross-cultural friendship. I had the opportunity of meeting a 19-year-old man named Adam. Developing a relationship with him was the epitome of this truth. It was work. We were two totally different people: he was an atheist, I was a Christian; he was from Hungary, I was from America; he was a communist, I was a capitalist; he spoke Hungarian, I spoke English. But because we were both "psyched up" to work at the relationship—it worked. We are friends to this day.

I mention this because I believe everyone of us shares in cross-cultural relationships each day of our lives—right here in the U.S. I am speaking of the differences between males and females. We represent two different cultures. We possess two different world views; we think and feel differently; and while we may use the same words, they may mean something totally different depending on who spoke them. I guess you could say we *do* speak different languages! What's more, we approach the art of mentoring differently. Yet, like my friendship with Adam, if we are prepared for this and are ready to work at understanding and enjoying the differences, we can actually benefit from each other. It can be a wonderful adventure in relationships.

In this chapter, I would like to communicate to you how mentoring is unique within the female gender. From my research with women and ministry among them, I will attempt to detail the natural, positive qualities they possess that spark healthy mentoring. I'll also point out some dangers they need to guard against. Clearly, men and women approach people and relationships differently. They embrace two diverse views of the subject and have distinctive tendencies based on their sexuality. Before I begin, let me give you a disclaimer. What you are about to read are generalizations. I am sure I have oversimplified the female gender in my attempt to fit the information into one chapter. I am also certain that you may know of exceptions to the "rules" I will communicate. However, I believe knowing this material will help you improve 80% of the mentoring mashaps that occur as you meet with the same sex. (I will do the same in the next chapter as I address the men). Let's begin with a simple chart or table that helps put this in perspective. It communicates our different emphases in mentoring:

WOMEN	MEN
1. Feelings	1. Thinking
2. Relationships	2. Results
3. Talking	3. Doing
4. Detail	4. Big Picture
5. Empathy	5. Problem Solving
6. Holistic	6. Categorical

Obviously, we can learn from each other. Men who focus on results, for instance, don't get very far unless they learn to build relationships along the way. Women, on the other hand, can end up chatting about a struggle in their life without ever getting to the answer. Each sex reveals a part of God that the other does not. My goal is for us to harvest the postive elements each gender has to offer. Let's take a moment to survey the positive qualities women share as they mentor.

POSITIVE QUALITIES WOMEN POSSESS

Before we examine the cautions and struggles we must resolve, let's take a look at why women do mentoring relationships well.

1. **Women draw their identity from the primary relationships in their lives.**
Women naturally bond because of their innate tendency to draw identity from others. For instance, God formed woman out of the rib of her husband in Genesis, and forever it has served as a word picture of how naturally women identify with the key people in their lives.

2. **Women enjoy being transparent and vulnerable.**
You usually don't have to tell women to open up and be transparent in conversation. In fact, quite the opposite is true. Women tend to draw fulfillment from their ability to share each other's pain and hardships and actually feel stronger by sharing weaknesses.

Men, on the other hand, generally do not feel safe sharing their weaknesses.

3. **Women are generally good at communication or are willing to work at it.**
In most cases, the women I know are good at interpersonal communication. In the few cases where they are not, they have

the capacity and are willing to work at it until they become effective. This is definitely not true for most men.

4. Women are willing to be interdependent with each other.

Most women are not loners. They usually don't have to face the challenge of overcoming independence to the same degree as men. Women are willing to say, "I need help!" and are open to direct accountability. It does not signify failure for them just because they can't do it on their own. Making it on their own has no great appeal to women.

5. Women are often more diligent encouragers.

This is not to say that men don't encourage each other. However, because men are often "bottom line" oriented, they may tend to offer one word of encouragement and expect the recipient to remember it for quite a while. Women don't seem to tire of offering constant words of encouragement to each other, knowing they need it themselves.

CAUTIONS FOR WOMEN WHO MENTOR

In order for this chapter to be genuinely helpful, we must look at the hurdles women will jump if they are to succeed at mentoring relationships. This next list represents the cautions I offer to women as they mentor:

1. *Because women focus so strongly on bonding relationally, they can prevent themselves from reaching the results they are after.* The emphasis on simply getting together and relating, conversing, and sharing may keep women from getting to a goal in their mentoring process.

2. *Because women empathize so well, they can foster unhealthy reliances in which mentees look to them, rather*

than to the Lord, for answers. I have watched women in discipleship relationships create a dependence on each other rather than on the Lord, since it is so much easier to bond to a friend than to an unseen Savior. Truly healthy mentoring is not finished until the mentee knows how to lean on the Lord.

3. *Because women enjoy the details of life, they can easily miss the "big picture."* It is easy for women to enter a conversation and become so engrossed with the little details, sharing "verbal detours" about their day, their family, their hassles, that they lose sight of the main issue—why they've committed to meeting in the first place.

4. *Because women are so relational, they can neglect the necessary structure needed to follow through on an objective.* With women, as with men, their strength is often their weakness. They have mastered the relationship part of mentoring so well that they can avoid, with disdain, the very system or structure needed to keep them on track with their initial goals.

5. *Because women value relationships so highly, those relationships can be a source of comparison and competition.* Women must guard against comparing personal features, personal friendships, personal focuses, and personal finesse with each other. They must remember that we will always find someone who is more beautiful, more poised socially, more talented, going a different direction and whose life appears more attractive.

6. *Because women build friendships so quickly, they can often take on too many relationships at too deep a level.* Intimacy can be invited much too quickly for many women. They can tend to "rescue" others and simply attract so many

deep relationships that they become overwhelmed. They must learn to plan ahead and establish boundaries within their relationships.

7. *Because relationships are so important, women can be tempted to control them.* Since women hold relationships so closely, they are prone to be controlling and force the direction they go and how deeply they progress. For instance, God told Eve in Genesis 3, that part of her curse would be to "yearn for control" of her husband. This is a battle women must fight and a temptation they must overcome.

8. *Because women enjoy talking over issues, they can overlook their vision for the future due to a tendency to hash out the past and present.* One practice that brings relief for most women is talking over problems—even if they don't arrive at a solution. This makes it easy for the mentoring session to focus merely on struggles and mutual misery instead of looking ahead and making tomorrow better.

9. *Because women relate through verbal conversation, they may tend to turn their mentoring meeting into a "chat" session that is not purpose driven.* This caution is closely related to the previous one. I believe mentoring happens best on purpose, not by accident. This means we cannot lose sight of our purpose as we meet together. Women must be conscious of the need to stay mission driven.

SOME TIPS FOR WOMEN WHO MENTOR

I trust that some of these insights have been helpful. I am indebted to my wife, a godly woman and mentor to many; Nancy Hensley, who has led a number of women's groups and discipleship ministries; Sheryl Fleisher, who led a large, churchwide women's discipleship ministry for over a decade; and others who gave input on compiling these tidbits. Now that we have observed the distinctives of the female gender, examined the positive qualities they possess, and surveyed the cautions they need to heed, let's close with a simple list of tips. These are practical steps I would advise most women to take to accentuate their *gender gifts!* These principles will help them play to their strengths and work on their weaknesses as they enter mentoring relationships:

1. Create a set routine, rhythm and schedule for mentoring. Deliberately insert structure into the relationship that will allow you to be relational, yet stay on track with where your are going. We need systems in our ministries to keep them progressing and to ensure they go beyond one generation. Plan both the time to meet and the goals to pursue.

2. Use a "tool" for mentoring. By a "tool" I simply mean a study guide or a book or some practical help that will take you where you want to go. Remember, you may be in a small group ministry in your church and not do anything but fellowship each week. In a mentoring relationship, by definition, you want to reach your potential, not just fellowship. Select a mentoring tool that will help you reach the specific goals you set.

3. Keep the end in mind and the goal before your eyes. Since you do relationships naturally, you won't need to work as hard on that component of mentoring. Instead you will need to remind each other of the goals you've set, and even maintain a list of the objectives in front of you at each meeting.

4. Work together to reinforce your identity in Christ, not in human status. Your identity does not come from comparing yourself to other women, even when that may be a natural temptation. You must hold each other accountable to reinforce where your identity should be drawn from—your position in Him.

5. Make prayer a priority in your mentoring relationship. While men need to do this to prevent them from self-sufficiency (looking to themselves), women need to make prayer a priority to prevent them from others-sufficiency (looking to each other). You must work at not looking to people (mentors) for the ultimate answers—but to the Lord.

How are Men Unique In Mentoring?

It dawned on me sometime during the summer of 1989. My wife and I had celebrated eight years of marriage together, but it had just struck me how differently she and I approach life and ministry. I had become serious about providing spiritual leadership in our home. I defined a spiritual leader as *one who assumes responsibility for the health and development of their relationships.* With this in mind, I had begun to negotiate with my wife, Pam, just how I could enhance her personal development. How could I help her grow? How could I mentor her spiritually?

After setting some goals together, I determined we'd reach those goals as strategically and swiftly as I knew how. I wanted to get her from Point A to Point B in a fluid manner; my pathway was to be the shortest distance between two points. It was then that I recognized we were pursuing our mutual goals in an entirely different fashion. Our conscious, intentional mentoring experiment came to a grinding halt. She was enjoying the process, while I could only find enjoyment in accomplishing the purpose. Looking back, I now realize that she was merely being herself, and I, myself. Neither of us was right or wrong. I was simply being a man, and she was being a woman. The grinding and polishing that takes place in a marriage often happens because of these very differences.

It is these differences between males and females that I've chosen to examine as they relate to the fine art of mentoring. In response to the previous chapter on the unique qualities and approaches women bring to a relationship, I want to offer some insights for men as well. Like the ladies, I believe men provide some positive qualities as they participate in the art of mentoring. They incarnate certain principles that make for a rich and wonderful experience. In addition, there are also some pitfalls they will likely face. I will offer cautions to the men and then close the chapter with some practical tips they should implement.

Let's begin the way we did the last chapter—with a simple table of the primary differences between men and women in the practice of mentoring. The following two columns reveal the differing emphases men and women usually embrace:

WOMEN		MEN	
1.	Feelings	1.	Thinking
2.	Relationships	2.	Results
3.	Talking	3.	Doing
4.	Detail	4.	Big Picture
5.	Empathy	5.	Problem Solving
6.	Holistic	6.	Categorical

As I mentioned in the chapter on women, we can learn from each other. Neither of these two columns is always right or always wrong. Men need to adopt more of the natural female tendencies, and vice versa. There should be a combination of both thinking and feeling; relationship and results; empathy and problem solving, etc. Now that we have briefly examined the female side, let's survey the men. I'd like to begin with a simple list of the positive qualities men naturally bring into the mentoring experience.

POSITIVE QUALITIES MEN POSSESS

Although both genders own more good characteristics than I can share in one chapter, let me zero in on five primary elements that men bring to the mentoring process.

1. Men enjoy getting down to business and reaching goals.
Men don't have too much problem cutting through the fat and getting to the bottom line of what needs to happen to improve a situation. What they often need is some empathy to accompany their diagnosis and prescription for each other. Men often size up a situation and offer a number of ways to reach an objective before their mentee can say, "Do you understand my question?"

2. Men can maintain their vision for the big picture.
Although women are much more holistic in their perspective, they can get lost easily in one particular issue during a conversation. Men, while they think in categories, seem to naturally be able to see each category as it relates to the "big picture." Again, they're good at seeing the "bottom line." This helps them to remain objective and solve problems for themselves and each other.

3. Men like action and generally don't waste time or words.
Have you ever heard a wife say about her husband, "He just doesn't communicate enough"? This frequently happens when the husband is stewing over a problem; he hibernates in his own world until he can think of a solution. This can be both bad and good. The good component to this tendency is that men want to actually *do something,* not just talk about it. They will often use a few choice words and then move toward the goal.

4. Men are natural problem solvers.
Clearly, this depends upon whether the subject even interests

them, but if it does, they will think long and hard about how to resolve any dilemmas they face. If the issue is of primary concern, they can be extremely creative and offer tremendous ingenuity. This may go back to the Garden of Eden when God chose Adam to manage it. God built man with an innate interest in managing his territory (responsibility) and his productivity.

5. Men can often remain logical and objective.

No doubt, there is a point in both genders when we can feel overwhelmed, and panic strikes like a snake. However, because men are better at thinking than feeling, they are able to limit how much their emotions control them as they face a problem. Temperaments within both sexes will also play a role in this, but the average man usually prides himself on being logical and objective—even in crisis.

WHY MEN STRUGGLE WITH RELATIONSHIPS

Later in this handbook, I will make a case for the primacy of relationships within our Christian faith. Our faith is not about mentally embracing creeds or doctrines, as is the case with other religions. It is about relationships: a vertical one with God, and a horizontal one with people. Remember the two greatest commandments? (Matthew 22:36-40) Jesus taught that we cannot separate our spiritual life (and depth) from our relationships with others. He didn't say, "By this will all men know that you are my disciples—because you have memorized seventy-five verses of scripture!" Instead, he said: "By this will all men know that you are my disciples, that you love one another."

The irony of all of this is that, in our Western culture, men very often make their religion simply one category of their lives. They frequently don't allow their faith to impact how they approach the other categories of their lives. They may be in church on Sunday, then cuss at their employees on Monday and not even see a problem with this. Unfortunately, although men don't "do" relationships as naturally as women, they must learn to prioritize them, and begin to become more like Jesus. The category that counted most to Him was people and relationships. What's more, we simply cannot do mentoring well if we don't do relationships well.

So why don't many men do relationships well? Is it just part of the curse of our sexuality? Are we destined to simply be stereotypes of John Wayne or James Bond or even Tim "the tool man" Taylor? I don't think so. However there are some hurdles we will have to jump if we are going to excel in relationships. The following list contains some cautions that men need to be aware of, especially as they begin to mentor others. The list details why men struggle with relationships. You will notice that this list includes elements from both nature and nurture. Let's look at them before I provide you with some tips to implement.

1. Men draw their identity more from achievement than from relationships. If you think about both the creation and the curse of man, we can clearly see the idea of *conquest* and achievement. While women draw their identity from *connection* to their world, the masculine gender draws it from conquest of their world. God told Adam to rule the earth; then, as part of his curse, God told him that now it would be done by the sweat of his brow. Both creation and curse were tied to his identity as a conqueror and achiever.

2. Men are tempted to stay at their workplace where they get training and strokes. Nearly every working man would say that he's received some training at his workplace. Almost the same percentage will say they've received no training whatsoever at their relationships—even when they've attended a Christian college. "Forgiveness 101" or "Listening Skills and Conflict Resolution" would be tremendously helpful courses for males, but are absent from our formal training. Furthermore, because the male usually performs well at the workplace, he gets strokes from his boss, his secretary or his foreman. Conversely, when he gets home, he may get nagged, since he is not doing so well there. Men are humans. Where do you think they are tempted to linger? As this all-too-common scenario was birthed, so was the proverbial "workaholic."

3. *Our culture is mistaken with its masculine image.* In my book, *Soul Provider*, I talk about the masculine image that has prevailed in America for decades. This image can be summarized with the words: strong, silent, self-sufficient, resourceful, shrewd and, on a good day, courteous to women and to each other. This image is typified by media personalities like John Wayne, Sean Connery (James Bond), Sylvester Stallone (Rocky), and Tim Allen (Tim Taylor). The images are: the cowboy, the playboy, the he-man, and the funny man. None is especially good at opening up emotionally. None is available for vulnerable and transparent accountability. Like it or not, these images have prevailed in real life as well.

4. *Men have rarely had good models of developmental relationships.* Few of us had patient mentors in our formative years. In addition, many of us never had fathers who knew how to be spiritual leaders in our homes. This left us with little more than books on the subject. We lacked a model who demonstrated what this should look like. Due to our lack of models, men often feel like fakes when it comes to authentic Christianity. When this is true, they either compensate by simply shutting down their emotions and communication, or swing to the other extreme and become overly flamboyant and demonstrative, searching for laughs or applause as an affirmation that they're OK.

5. Men are driven to get to the bottom line and not oriented to enjoying the process. Still another pitfall is that men are frequently impatient when it looks like progress is not being made fast enough. We want to race to the results; we want to see the product in our hands. This tendency is fostered by our American corporate culture. Unfortunately, men must experience a paradigm shift if they are to be effective mentors. Mentoring is frequently a slow process. God shapes mentees in a crockpot, not a microwave oven.

6. Men prefer pure action over conversation. This is both goods news and bad news. The masculine strength is also our weakness. We want action. But, we often want it at the expense of building good, deep relationships with others. We'd rather not hear about someone's personal affairs if it is going to take too long, and keep us from another item on our "to do" list. Men need to learn to enjoy pure communication and conversation. That is not to say there should be no action. But results without relationship don't impress God. Men must learn to relate and identify with others. God saves people, not projects.

7. Men don't feel safe being vulnerable and revealing their feelings. Still another reason why relationships are difficult for men is that they don't share their honest feelings very freely. Perhaps this is a safeguard. Women often share them too freely. Men, however, must learn to be transparent and determine to build safe places to be vulnerable – with a mentee or a handful of other men in an accountability group.

8. Men want to see tangible results quickly. This is a second cousin to number five, above. Not only do men appear too busy to just enjoy the journey, but they want to see visible, tangible, measurable results...fast. If they don't physically see progress, they can become discouraged, since their masculinity is driven by accomplishment. Unfortunately, good mentoring requires intimacy, and intimacy doesn't happen overnight. Most of the time, men will have to trim back on their expectations and learn to set mini-goals. Perhaps we need to allow our mentees to make mini-decisions so that we can enjoy the process from week to week.

9. *Men can be self-sufficient.* Finally, men must overcome their tendency to be self-reliant if they are to become effective in the relationship/mentoring business. We need to recognize that we really do need each other. Interdependence is a quality that comes naturally to most women. Men must make conscious decisions to disclose their weakness and, sometimes, even let a mentee help them. One of the best ways a man can affirm and communicate value to others is to *need them* and the help they can give.

SOME TIPS FOR MEN WHO MENTOR

Allow me to close this chapter by listing some practical hints that just might make you, as a male, a better mentor to others. These are based upon the insights we've just reviewed together. See what you think:

1. Plan events together just for the sake of the relationship. In order to revolt against the temptation to race to the solution without relishing the journey, try planning some *relational* time together without discussing a deep spiritual insight or setting some lofty goal. Let your hair down and let them see you do it. Insert a regular rhythm of these friendship times, knowing that they help you earn the right to speak into their lives.

2. Create safe places for transparent communication. You may need to begin by asking for their forgiveness for your failure to model transparency and vulnerability. Once you have articulated this goal, find a place where you believe you can open up and share. Very likely, you will need to get away from the coffee shop or other public places. Write down and discuss your secret longings, your sins or your personal aspirations—then, pray together about them.

3. Find models of intimacy and healthy male friendships. If neither of you had good models of masculine intimacy and accountability, you may want to seek out other men who exemplify this quality. It might be good to sit down and interview this "model" together and learn side by side. Healthy relationships are more *caught than taught.* You need to be "exposed" to them for a season.

4. Make healthy intimacy one of your goals. If you feel you fall into the category of a typical male, and love setting goals for yourself, then may I suggest you make "relationship" one of your goals. Set an objective for a level of intimacy that is measurable and achievable, then pursue it with a passion. Read about it in books, listen to other men on the subject, and then discuss it together. If you want it badly enough, you'll get it. Give each other permission to be held accountable.

5. Make prayer a priority. This was one of the tips I also gave to the women. However, I give it to you for a different reason. Obviously, both genders need to learn dependence upon God. Women need to because they are prone to become reliant upon each other as human sources of answers. Men, on the other hand, need to prioritize prayer because they are prone to become self-reliant; they reach down into their own human reservoirs and artificially conjure up the juices to make it happen all by themselves. Praying together in a mentoring relationship enables you to include both another person and your Lord in the solution.

How Do I Find A Mentor?

It was wise advice when someone once said: "Everyone needs a mentor, including mentors."

Each of us should always be looking to someone who is a step ahead of us in life; someone who helps us examine our habits, our schedules, our thoughts, our feelings and our results. This chapter will address how to find such a person.

RECOGNIZE WHAT YOU ARE LOOKING FOR

As you seek a mentor, you must understand what it is you are looking for—or you may not recognize them when you meet them. Keep in mind, mentors are not. . .

- perfect people
- leaders who try to make you like them
- workers who want to use you to help accomplish their goals
- people who give you time out of duty and obligation
- successes who will give you a "free ride" to fame and fortune

Instead, mentors are humans, just like you, who are further along in life (maturity) and have chosen to make "deposits" in others. Mentors are genuine, giving, caring, insightful and secure people. Author Bob Biehl once said:

- ♦ **MENTORS** are more like caring aunts and uncles than like another mother or father.

- ♦ **MENTORS** are those with whom we
  share the lows
  and
  celebrate the highs in life. . .
  together!

- ♦ **MENTORS** are those rare individuals in life who
  love us deeply. . .
  see our greatest potentials. . .
  cheer us on. . .
  correct when needed. . .
  teach us selflessly about life. . .
  become our lifelong friends. . .
  at whose funerals
  we weep unashamedly. . .
  with no regard whatsoever for the clock.

It is my prayer that every person who reads this handbook finds such a person. In order for that to happen, you must take some initial steps.

TAKING THE FIRST STEP

Often I encourage a young adult to seek out a mentor. When I do, they are frequently convinced that there are none anywhere near them. They claim their church has no one with any spiritual depth or with any time. They contend their town is too small, or the generation gap is too wide to connect with someone closely. There are simply none to be found.

In such a case, I generally recommend that the young adult begin to pray consistently about the issue. Daily, perhaps. I am constantly amazed, when I become fervent in prayer over a request, how often God surprises me with an answer right under my nose. You may be amazed to find that a potential mentor already exists nearby, but you didn't have the "eyes" to see them.

A second step, once you've begun praying, is to lower your standard. Perhaps you're looking for an ideal mentor that truly doesn't exist. . .anywhere in the world. Take what you can get.

Third, be willing to sacrifice to find them. This may mean driving a couple of hours to meet with them each month. It could mean you are to meet with someone each month face to face, and to add a second or third person that you correspond with, via the mail, who adds some dimensions to the mentoring that the face-to-face person doesn't possess. That's fine, too.

Finally, keep your antennas up. Everywhere you go in your daily routines, be on the lookout for potential mentors. Stay conscious of the value that each person you meet adds to your life. Mentors are everywhere if you just stop and think about it.

CHOOSING A MENTOR

When you are ready to approach a potential mentor, be ready to do most of the work. Dr. Ted Engstrom recommends that you keep the following list in mind.

1. Ask him or her to help you ask the right questions, search in the right places, and stay interested in the right answers.

2. Decide what degree of excellence or perfection you want. Generally the object of mentoring is improvement, not perfection. Perhaps only a few can be truly excellent—but all can be better.

3. Accept a subordinate, learning position. Don't let ego get in the way of learning or try to impress the mentor with your knowledge or ability and thus set up a mental barrier against taking in as fast it's being given out.

4. Respect the mentor but don't idolize him. Respect allows us to accept what he or she is teaching—but making the mentor an idol removes our critical faculty for fitting a mentor's thinking to ourselves.

5. Put into effect immediately what you are learning. The best mentoring is intensity in a narrow field. Learn, practice, and assimilate.

6. Set up a discipline for relating to the mentor. Arrange for an ample and consistent time schedule, select the

   subject matter in advance, and do your homework to make the sessions profitable.

7. Reward your mentor with your own progress. If you show appreciation but make no progress, the mentor knows he's failed. Your progress is his highest reward.

8. Learn to ask crucial questions—questions that prove you have been thinking between sessions, questions that show progress in your perception.

9. Don't threaten to give up. Let your mentor know that you have made a decision for progress, that he is dealing with a persistent person—a determined winner. Then he knows he is not wasting his time.

SET YOUR GOALS

Over the last several years I have attempted to match up hundreds of mentoring relationships within the church. Because the college students with whom I have worked varied so greatly in their maturity and interests, I came up with a simple formula to help them all find a suitable mentor. You might say I crystallized the bare essentials of a mentor; I reduced the criteria to the lowest common denominator. It became the goal for each student who sought a mentor. Interestingly, the elements actually spell the word GOALS:

G - GODLINESS - They must demonstrate godly character and conduct that is worth imitating. They should remind you of Jesus.

O - OBJECTIVITY - They must be able to see strengths and weaknesses clearly, and be willing to communicate those honestly.

A - AUTHENTICITY - They must be real. You must be able to see their humanity; they should be genuine, transparent and open with you.

L - LOYALTY- They must be people who are loyal to others. When friendships (or mentoring relationships) are formed, they are committed to them.

S - SERVANTHOOD - They must be willing to give generously of their time, resources and wisdom. They see their mentee as a big part of their ministry.

Why not set out on your pursuit of a mentor with this "blueprint" in mind? You will probably find that potential mentors possess several other qualities that will enrich your life, but these five lay a great foundation for producing a healthy relationship.

Remember: seeking mentors is a biblical practice. The Apostle Paul exhorted young women to seek the mentoring of older women, and he encouraged young men to seek it from older men. Even King Solomon encouraged it thousands of years ago in the scripture. The following are some proverbs paraphrased from his writings:

Counsel in another's heart is like deep water, but a discerning man will draw it up.

Proverbs 20:5

A straightforward answer is as good as a kiss of friendship.

Proverbs 24:26

As iron sharpens iron, so one man sharpens the wit of another.

Proverbs 27:17

A CHECKLIST

To conclude this chapter I want to provide a checklist for finding and choosing a mentor. Before you make the decision, check to see if he or she has these qualities:

♦ Will the mentor be an objective, lovingly honest, and balanced source of feedback for your questions?
♦ Will the mentor be open and transparent with their own struggles?
♦ Will the mentor model their teachings?
♦ Does the mentor know and believe in you. . .one of your chief cheerleaders and not your chief critic?
♦ Will the mentor teach as well as answer your questions?
♦ Is the mentor successful in your eyes?
♦ Will the mentor be open to two-way communication... learning from you on occasion as well as teaching you?
♦ Does the mentor want to see younger people succeed in developing their spiritual and leadership potential?

A final note: Refer to the "Mentor Match-up" form I provide in Chapter 16. This helpful little profile will enable you to locate the appropriate mentor or mentee that fits *your* personality, style and goals.

How Do I Find
A Mentee?

When you are ready to invest your life in someone else, the first question you'll face is: WHO? In whom should I regularly make deposits? How will I know if I've chosen someone wisely? Is there some kind of guideline that can help me make this decision?

In the next few pages I'll attempt to outline the answers to these questions. I believe we ought to pray for a "divine appointment," as a first step, when it comes to our mentee. After all, that's what Jesus did first. However, apart from God's direct intervention, there are some wisdom principles, (some of them directly from scripture) that we can employ in our decision.

YOU MUST LOOK FOR "FAITH"

Over the last several years I have mentored dozens of interns who committed two years to our internship program at the church. The inner qualities I looked for in potential interns (mentees) can be summarized in the acrostic: FAITH.

F - FAITHFUL

Is this person faithful to commitments they've made, as well as to the basics of the Christian faith?

A - AVAILABLE

Does this person have the time, and do they make themselves available to growth opportunities as a priority?

I - INITIATIVE

Do they show initiative in their desire to grow? Are they willing to take the first step without someone "holding their hand?"

T - TEACHABLE

Is this person willing to learn new truths and be open to change? Do they exhibit a "soft" or a stubborn heart? Will they learn from you?

H - HUNGRY

Does this person have a passion to grow and be all they can be for God? Do they hunger for intimacy with God?

If you can find a person who meets each of these criteria, it will be difficult to make a bad decision. Memorize the FAITH acrostic and keep the questions in mind.

MENTORING POTENTIAL LEADERS

If you are committed to mentoring only potential leaders, those who will influence people and organizations, then you may want to include an additional acrostic in your criteria: GIFT or SHARP:

G - GIFTS

Do they exhibit some obvious gifts for ministry or leadership? Do they have the aptitude and potential to be a key influencer wherever they go in the future?

I - INFLUENCE

Are they already influencing their peers and the groups with whom they associate? Are they often influenced by others or do they, instead, leave their mark on others?

F - FAVOR

How much do people favor them? Are they liked and respected by others and seem to have God's hand on their life/ministry? Is God's anointing on them?

T - TRUSTWORTHY

Do they seem credible with their life and leadership? With all the gifts they have, is their character as deep as their gifts? Can they be trusted with responsibility?

Still another acrostic you may want to use for selecting a mentee is SHARP. It asks some similar but more fundamental questions about the person's character:

S - SERVING

Are they already serving in some area of ministry? Are they active and involved in the church, or are they waiting for someone to tell them where to turn?

H - HUNGRY

As I've already mentioned, you must ask whether they are hungry to stretch and grow from new experiences and truths.

A - APTITUDE

Do they exhibit an aptitude for ministry? Are they good thinkers? Do they reflect and act strategically when they get involved?

R - RELIABLE

Do you consider them to be reliable with any instruction or request they receive? Do they show a faithful spirit to the things they already know to do?

P - POTENTIAL

Are they high-potential people? Can you see God's vision for them and a passion to impact others for the Kingdom? Do you feel certain they will reproduce what you give them?

Paul Stanley reminds us of an additional component to the decision. "Mentoring is an empowering experience that requires a connection between two people...the mentor and the mentoree. Factors such as time, proximity, needs, shared values, and goals affect any relationship. But the mentoring relationship needs three additional factors, or dynamics, to bring about empowerment. These dynamics are constantly at play in the context of a mentoring relationship and directly affect the mentoree's progress, change, and level of empowerment.

"The following dynamics are vital to the mentoring relationship:

1. *Attraction*-This is the necessary starting point in the mentoring relationship. The mentoree is drawn to the mentor for various reasons: perspective, certain skills, experience, value and commitments modeled, perceived wisdom, position, character, knowledge, and influence. The mentor is attracted to the mentoree's atti-

tude, potential, and opportunity for influence. As attraction increases, trust, confidence, and mentoring subjects develop that will strengthen the mentoring relationship and ensure empowerment.

2. *Responsiveness*-The mentoree must be willing and ready to learn from the mentor. Attitude is crucial for the mentoree. A responsive, receiving spirit on the part of the mentoree and attentiveness on the part of the mentor directly speed up and enhance the empowerment.

3. *Accountability*-Mutual responsibility for one another in the mentoring process ensures progress and closure. Sharing expectations and a periodic review and evaluation will give strength to application and facilitate empowerment. The mentor should take responsibility for initiating and maintaining accountability with the mentoree.

"The more deliberate and intense the mentoring relationship, the more important these dynamics are. Why is this true? Because mutual commitment is necessary for change and growth to take place. These dynamics are the ingredients that produce this commitment."

Because of these dynamics, the selection of your mentee becomes a crucial decision. Please make it prayerfully and carefully. Sociologists tell us that the most introverted individual will influence 10,000 other people during an average lifetime. Wow! Imagine what kind of influence we might have if we actually pray and choose those individuals intentionally.

COMMON QUESTIONS ON MENTORING

Gleaning from the wisdom of such men as Ted Engstrom, Bobb Biehl, Howard Hendricks, John Maxwell, Robert Clinton and Paul Stanley, the following list of questions and answers are provided for your benefit. Read them over carefully.

◆ Where does mentoring happen?

Everywhere. Most mentoring takes place in a very relaxed setting as it did centuries ago in *fatherly apprenticeships*...walking, sailing, golfing, driving...anywhere you are with your mentor or your mentee.

Mentoring often happens ten minutes at a time...here and there as you move through life together. Don't see mentoring as all work. *It often involves the joy of mutual sharing. Mentoring happens more in the context of a relationship than a formal classroom.* Mentoring is a life attitude as much as a formal structure. It can be even more enjoyable as you are doing things you enjoy together!

◆ At what age do you want to begin mentoring someone?

At the age where they have clear goals they want to reach. This may begin around age 16 or, in some situations, even a little earlier.

◆ What difference does age play in the mentoring process?

Age is not as large a factor as experience and maturity. Sometimes the mentor is actually a few years younger than the protege. However, if you were to take all of the mentors in the world, I'd estimate that most would be 5-20 years older than the mentees.

◆ What happens when a mentee or mentor fails?

No mentee wants to fail, but sometimes they need a mentor's help to know how to succeed. . .and how to learn from failure. A wise mentor expects a mentee to be less than perfect, especially in the formative years. A mentee should have NO FEAR OF BEING REJECTED by the mentor. It is also helpful for the mentor and mentee to discuss failure, including the freedom to fail and not be rejected, before the inevitable failure occurs.

No mentor wants to fail. A wise mentee expects a mentor to be less than perfect. A mentor should also have NO FEAR OF BEING REJECTED by the mentee.

◆ Does a mentor have to be perfectly mature, an ideal model of the Christian faith and an extreme success, to be a mentor?

No. . .no mentor is perfect! Each mentor only needs to be stronger in some areas than the mentee in order to be a big help. At the same time, if the mentor has a major problem, it is difficult to lead a mentee in this area. That is why, ideally, each mentor also has one or more mentors.

◆ What effect does a mentee's motivation level have on a mentor?

The more eager a mentee is to learn, the more eager the mentor is to teach!

◆ Can a man mentor a woman, or a woman mentor a man?

Most studies indicate that in business today, many men mentor both men and women. At the same time, many women mentor both sexes.

In Scripture the primary references, as in Titus 2:4-5, are to older women helping younger women and, in II Timothy 2:2, to older men helping younger men.

The relationship between the mentor and the mentee typically becomes emotionally intimate. Therefore, the mentee and mentor relationship is POTENTIALLY very dangerous to have with the opposite sex outside of marriage.

IT IS NOT RECOMMENDED!

♦ **What role does accountability play in the mentor/ mentee relationship?**
The main reason for accountability is to help mentees reach spiritual maturity and to develop their full leadership potential. Mentors must hold the mentees accountable, not on a daily or weekly basis, but as needed and agreed upon. The frequency and level of accountability will vary greatly with each mentee.

Note: It is important to remember that all accountability is ultimately to God. Just because a mentor will let you get by with something does not mean that God will. Just because a mentor feels something is okay does not mean that God does. Just because you can successfully hide something from the mentor who is holding you accountable does not mean it is hidden from God.

So also, mentors are not accountable for the success of their mentees. Mentors can help mentees succeed in reaching their goals. . .but the responsibility for reaching goals always remains clearly with the mentees.

♦ **How confident do most people feel about becoming mentors?**
Most of the adults I have met feel somewhat intimidated by the word MENTORING. However, most people do not realize

how effective they could be. Their fears prevent them from seeing their possibilities.

At the same time, most adults can quickly name three young people who could benefit from their support and encouragement. Most people say they would have benefited from such a supportive relationship in their life or, in fact, did while they were younger.

Whatever you do, don't let a little discomfort keep you from approaching one to three high potential young people and offering your mentoring support. They need your experience, wisdom and encouragement!

♦ **What difference does mentoring make over a lifetime?**

Mentoring can make an extremely significant difference in a leader's lifetime achievements. Often one timely idea or a single word of encouragement influences a young leader to hang in there. One simple cup-of-coffee conversation at a critical time may shape a young leader's entire life direction. Wisely shared perspective can build faith, sustain courage, and lead to visionary change and powerful accomplishments for God's kingdom.

Many suicide notes say something like, "When I needed help, no one seemed to care about me personally...I was all alone...no one cares if I live or die!" As rare as physical suicide may be, spiritual, career, and family suicides are quite common. However, with a mentor in place who loves the mentee, this is rarely the case. Therefore, in some situations mentoring is actually the critical link to life.

Ask yourself this simple question: What difference would a

sharp, caring mentor have made in my life at an early age? What if someone had approached you and said, "I really believe in you. In fact, I care about you so much, I'd like to meet with you and do everything in my power to make sure you succeed at your goals. I am going to ask you two simple questions each meeting: 'What are your priorities?' and 'How can I help?' I think your life is going to make a difference in the world, and I want to help empower you to reach your potential!" Now—don't you think that would have made a difference in what you attempted as a young adult?

♦ **Does a mentor/mentee relationship last for a life time?**

Ideally yes!. . .But realistically. . .seldom. It is best to agree upon a set time (six months to a year) and then evaluate. At that point you can decide whether to stop or continue.

Occasionally the relationship changes as the mentor moves away. Occasionally the relationship changes as the needs of the mentee change in different life phases. Occasionally conflict arises and the relationship simply stops. Most typically, the mentoring *friendship* lasts a lifetime.

♦ **What happens when the mentee outgrows the mentor?**

Frequently...great pain comes into the mentor and mentee relationship, and a broken relationship occurs.

Ideally...the relationship changes from mentor/mentee to friends, and mentors are honored to see their mentees succeed—much as fathers and mothers are honored by the success of their children in adulthood. Mentors must be secure in their own identity for this to occur.

♦ **What happens if my mentor or mentee doesn't follow through with our original agreement?**
First of all. . .STAY POSITIVE!

Assume the mentor or mentee wants to get together but is just busy. Take the initiative. Don't wait and let your fears and anxiety build. Probably just a difference of assumptions or a busy schedule is the problem, not a personal reason.

You are not being rejected!

You may need to redefine your relationship to require less time or a different time that is better for both of your schedules. Don't give up; just redefine. (See Chapter 8 for details.)

A CHECKLIST

It's wise to have in mind the kind of mentee you're looking for before you begin searching for one. The following is a checklist to help you make a decision. Does the potential mentee possess these qualities?

- ♦ Will you be able to believe 100% in this person?
- ♦ Do you naturally enjoy communicating with this person?
- ♦ Will you be able to give without reservation to this person?
- ♦ Will you love him or her as a brother or sister?
- ♦ Do you admire their potential as a leader?
- ♦ Is this person teachable. . .eager to learn from you and mature in his or her spiritual and leadership potential?
- ♦ Does this person admire you?
- ♦ Is this person self-motivated even though not always confident?

♦ Will this person be threatened *by you* or threatening *to you?*

♦ Does this person have the time to meet regularly?

♦ Is God the first priority in their life?

STEPS TO EFFECTIVE MENTORING

1. Select a mentee whose philosophy of life you share. Our greatest mentors are those who are also our models.

2. Choose a person with potential you genuinely believe in. Some of the nation's greatest athletes have come from tiny schools that receive no publicity. All those ball players needed was for scouts to recognize the potential that great coaching could bring out. The secret of mentoring in any field is to help a person get to where he or she is willing to go.

3. Evaluate a mentee's progress constantly. An honest mentor will be objective. If necessary, he or she will encourage the mentee to stay on course, to seek another direction, or even to enter into a relationship with another mentor.

4. Be committed, serious, and available to mentees. New York Philharmonic Conductor Zubin Mehta said of a young pianist: "I cannot teach him how to play, for he knows what the composer wanted to say; I can simply help him say it."

NOTE: Please refer to the "Mentor Match-up" form in Chapter 16 to use as a guide for your decision.

WHAT IF MENTORING IS NEW TO ME?

The more I travel and speak on this subject, the more I'm discovering how *new* it is to the Church. It's not so much that the *idea* is unheard of—but the *practice* of actually entering into a developmental relationship is rare, indeed. We talk about mentoring more readily than we do it. For many, it is still a far off desire.

Most Christians I meet still feel like they need to be mentored. Regardless of their age, gender, marital status, vocation or ministry experience—the majority of the evangelicals I come in contact with perceive themselves to be a "Timothy" looking for a "Paul." I recently spoke in New York and met a sharp gentleman that I guessed to be about 65 years old. He had participated in church events all his life, had served on almost every committee in his home church, and had been a leader in that church for as long as he could remember. Yet as we interacted following the morning worship service, I saw a hunger in his eyes for what I had spoken about; he was crying out for a mentor! He asked me what I thought he should do.

I'm not sure if my answer provided much comfort for him. I told him I would pray with him for appropriate mentor(s) to come beside him. I also reminded him to discard the notion that one "perfect" mentor would come along and eliminate his quest for answers. In fact, most often God provides our answers through the voices of several mentors, some of whom might be right under our noses, while others might live far away and require lengthy phone conversations. Again, we need to be open to redefine our stereotypes of mentors.

Following that exhortation, I added these words, which I direct to you as well: whatever you *do* possess, spiritually—pass it on now! In other words, if we wait to be mentored before we feel equipped to spiritually reproduce, we'll never get around to mentoring someone else! We will produce still one more generation fumbling through life and ministry in the dark! Yes, I agree it is pitiful that so many of us in the body of Christ have never been mentored; and yes, I agree we should be looking for that mentor as we progress through our journey. But, I fear that if we don't go ahead and give away the gifts we already have in our possession—via a mentoring relationship—what we will reproduce is another empty, wounded, disconnected and disappointed generation of people in the Church.

I love the story of the elderly gentleman who boarded a bus with a bouquet of flowers in his hand. As he sat down, he noticed an attractive young girl sitting across from him. Her eyes kept drifting over to the flowers. It was obvious that she was taken by them. In a few minutes it was time for the man to get off the bus. Standing to his feet, he handed the flowers to the girl and said, "I noticed that you like flowers. I would like for you to have these. I think my wife would like for you to have them, too. I'll tell her I gave them to you." With that, he stepped off the bus... and entered the gate of a small cemetery.

The beauty of the story is that the man gave the "gifts" that he had to someone who could use and appreciate them. Rather than dwelling on the past, he invested in the future. Gandhi, the famous Indian leader would have agreed with that gentleman's logic. One day, while boarding a train in India, he lost one of his sandals. As it tumbled to the tracks, Gandhi attempted to reach it—but failed. At that point, he did a strange thing. He removed his other sandal and tossed it on to the track next to the first one. When his fellow passengers asked him why he'd done it, he simply replied, "When some poor fellow finds that first sandal, now he'll have a pair he can wear."

HOW DO I APPROACH A POTENTIAL MENTORING RELATIONSHIP?

I am frequently struck by the simplicity of how Jesus selected his twelve disciples or mentees in the Gospels. It appears that He simply prayed all night, then chose a handful of men—from scratch! What's more, it seems as though they just up and left their work and followed Him, without any prior knowledge of what they were in for. Oh, if it were only that easy today, we sigh. If only we could find a mentor with that much authority and credibility; or, if only we could get people to follow our mentoring that quickly and simply.

Upon closer study we discover that it really *wasn't* that easy, even for Jesus. No doubt, there was a time when He did issue a challenge to Peter, James and John to follow Him, and they did, indeed, leave their nets to follow. I do not believe, however, that this was their first exposure to Jesus or His call on their lives. I believe there was a PROCESS involved that required several *stages* of relationship. My good friend Steve Moore and I have assigned titles to these stages of relationships to help you see the process necessary for people to make the kind of commitment that mentoring requires. I share this with you to liberate you from unrealistic expectations and to give you a path to take as you enter the process yourself. Let me outline it for you.

COME AND SEE...

This is stage one. In the Gospel of John, we see Jesus' first encounter with his potential disciples or mentees. In John 1:35-51, a conversation begins when Jesus discovers that two of John the Baptizer's disciples are following Him. He asks them what they are seeking. They inquire where He is staying. They are obviously at a **curiosity level.** They just want to know a little bit more about Him and what it means to be associated with Him. After all, this is a new experience. All He says in response is: "Come and see." For us, this may mean offering an opportunity to a potential mentee to observe some ministry in action, or to spend some time with us personally—just to get acquainted. If you are going to win their trust, you need to give them time. By offering these opportunities, you are demonstrating *first* your commitment and intentions to them. The commitment level is low, and the challenge is simple and easy. Your relationship may even be in its early stages. Your appropriate call on their life is simply: come and see.

COME AND FOLLOW...

This is stage two. At this stage, Jesus believes His disciples are ready to actually make a commitment, and follow after Him as a mentor. This is precisely what many of the twelve were after. Some of them, at this point, are not ready to call Him "Lord." He is "teacher" to them. In Luke 5:1-11, Simon Peter doesn't even feel comfortable being *close* to Jesus, and tells Him to depart from the area. Peter realized what an unworthy man he was, and that the Lord Himself was standing in front of him. Jesus knew he was ready for stage two, however, and simply said, "Do not fear, from now on you will be catching men." In Matthew 4:19, His words are put this way: "Come, follow me, and I will make you fishers of men." These kinds of words are to be spoken to those ready for the **commitment level,** who are ready to sacrifice in order to go forward and grow further. The word "follow" means "repeated, deliberate steps." Everyone is not ready for this level of commitment to a mentoring process. At this stage, mentees prove themselves to be faithful to the little tasks and assignments given by the mentor. They are willing to "follow the ruts of routine until they have become grooves of grace," as Dr. Vernon Grounds has put it. These routines might be faithfulness in meeting together, reading books that you will later discuss together, performing a ministry task, keeping a journal, fasting, etc. At this stage, the mentee is clearly prepared to deliberately follow the mentor.

COME AND SURRENDER...

This is stage three. Somewhere in the midst of Jesus' three-and-a-half-year ministry to the twelve, He issued a deeper challenge to them as mentees. In a word, you might say He asked them to "die"; to make the ultimate commitment. In Mark 8:34-35, He said: "If anyone wishes to come after Me, let him deny himself, take up his cross, and follow Me. For whoever wishes to save his life shall lose it; but whoever loses his life for My sake and the gospel's shall save it." This kind of call is appropriate for those at the **conviction level.** If a person is not ready to take this deep and heavy step, it will become clear by their reaction. Do you remember the rich young ruler? Jesus asked him to sell everything he had (something He did not ask of everyone He met) and to come follow Him. The young man, who thought he was further along in his spiritual journey than he was, just dropped his head and walked away. The step was too big for him to take.

At this stage, the mentee has so bought into the mentor that they not only love the mentor, but *their cause* as well. They are prepared to give their life to the mission. Profound steps of action can be expected from the mentee because the maturity level is deep. It is very appropriate, then, to issue a challenge: come and surrender.

COME AND MULTIPLY...

This is the fourth stage. During the latter part of Jesus' mentoring relationship with the twelve, He began to send them out to do it themselves. In fact, the final words He spoke to them are called "the Great Commission." In Matthew 28:19-20, we read: "Go and make disciples of all nations, baptizing them...and teaching them to obey all that I've commanded you..." In Mark 16, His words are: "Go into all the world and preach the Gospel to every creature..." In John 20:21, He said, "As the Father has sent Me, so I send you." They were to duplicate what He had just done with them as mentees. This is the **commissioned level.** We're to go full circle. At this point, the mentee is ready to become a mentor. If they are to continue stretching and growing, they must be "pushed out of the nest" and made to fly. They must pass on what they've received; they must imitate the process and duplicate the lifestyle. They must reproduce themselves. Unfortunately, very few ever reach this level. Many stop and are satisfied at merely being mentored. But Jesus said, "Freely you have received, freely give." He also issued this final call to us: come and multiply.

WHAT IS SUPPOSED TO HAPPEN IN A MENTORING RELATIONSHIP?

So—what is it we are called to do if we mentor someone else? Good question. Over the last several years I have made it my aim to distill the ingredients that make a good mentoring experience. The following word pictures represent what I believe are the most helpful goals you can shoot for as you attempt to invest in someone.

1. GIVE THEM "HANDLES"

Everyone possesses some knowledge of truth. Most people, however, are hard pressed to own it in such a way as to use it in everyday life. Simply put, "handles" are things we can grab on to. We give people "handles" when we summarize truths or principles in a user-friendly fashion. Truth, then, becomes a principle they can live by. When someone has a "handle" on something, it means they "own it" and can practice it as well as communicate it to others. A good mentor can distill or crystallize truth so that the *complex* becomes very *simple*.

For instance mentors may provide a "handle" for their mentees by summarizing the truth they are discussing into a brief phrase, slogan or jingle. They may choose to add a memorable experience together. A great lesson in servanthood can be learned by working in a soup kitchen downtown or by serving in a retirement home.

2. GIVE THEM "ROADMAPS"

Roadmaps give us direction in our journey and a view of the "big picture." When we give someone a "roadmap," we are passing on a life compass to them.

In the same way that maps help us travel on roads we've never been on, these spiritual roadmaps help people not only to see the right road, but to see that road in relation to all the other roads. They provide perspective on the whole picture. This generally happens only when we communicate *intentionally*, not *accidentally*. While there is a place for spontaneous interaction, planned opportunities to speak into a mentee's life are necessary. Fellowship may happen by chance, mentoring happens on purpose. We must be proactive about who we meet with and what we say to others.

3. GIVE THEM "LABORATORIES"

When we provide "laboratories" for our mentees, we are giving them a place to practice the truth we've discussed with them. Do you remember science class in college? They always included a lecture and a "lab." By definition, laboratories are safe places in which to experiment. We all need a "lab" to accompany all the "lectures" we get in the church. In these "labs," we learn the right questions to ask, the appropriate exercises to practice, an understanding of the issues, and experiential knowledge of what our agenda should be in life. Good laboratories are measurable; they have a beginning and an ending point; they can be evaluated together; and they provide ideas for life-application. In these labs mentors can supervise their mentees like a coach. They can oversee their experimentation like a professor. They can interpret life like a parent.

Every time I meet with my mentees, I have a "laboratory" idea to accompany the ministry principle I want them to learn. This forces me to be creative, but I believe in the axiom: spiritual information without spiritual application leads to spiritual constipation!

4. GIVE THEM "ROOTS"

One of the most crucial goals mentors ought to have for their mentees is to give them "roots and wings." This popular phrase describes everyone's need for foundations to be laid and for the freedom to soar and broaden their horizons. The foundation we must help to lay in our mentees involves the construction of a "character-based life" versus an "emotion-based life." They should leave us possessing strong convictions by which they can live their lives and the self-esteem to stand behind those convictions. The deeper the roots, the taller a tree can grow, and the more durable that tree is during a storm. If you are training someone for ministry—don't move on to heavy and glamorous subjects with them until they've mastered the basics—and have deep roots.

5. GIVE THEM "WINGS"

The final word picture that describes what a mentor must give a mentee is "wings." We give someone wings when we enable them to think big and expect big things from God and themselves. When someone possesses wings, they are free to explore and to plumb the depths of their own potential. When mentors give wings, they help mentees soar to new heights in their lives. Consequently, it's as important to teach them how to ask questions as how to obtain answers.

Mentors should empower mentees to take the limits off what they might accomplish with their lives—and be filled with joy when their mentees surpass their own level of personal achievement.

Dr. Howard Hendricks remembers a professor he had in college who continued to study and consume books late into his life. When he asked his prof why he spent so much time poring over his books, the instructor responded simply: "It is because I'd rather my students drink from a flowing stream than a stagnant pool."

This is the kind of mindset that fosters healthy and hungry mentees. When we provide handles, roadmaps, laboratories, roots and wings, we spawn strong, growing disciples who believe in their God and themselves. In John 1:17, we read that "grace and truth came through Jesus Christ." This is what empowers mentees—grace and truth. Grace is the relational love that knows no conditions; it is the warm, personal side of mentoring. Truth is the firm, steady, objective guide that provides a stable foundation for life. In other words mentors have a compass in their heads, and a magnet in their hearts.

Deanna was a high school student who always made good grades—until she took chemistry. Somehow she just didn't get it, no matter how hard she tried. As a matter of fact, she ended up failing the course. Fortunately, her teacher was also her mentor. He knew how devastating it would be to Deanna and her family to see an "F" on her report card. Still, he had to give her the grade. He vacillated over how to deal with the situation. Finally, he found the answer by offering both grace and truth. On her report card, he simply put an "F" next to the subject of Chemistry. However, on the same line he wrote these words: "We cannot all be chemists...but oh, how we would all love to be Deannas."

THE SEVEN GIFTS OF A MENTOR

All of us need mentors who can give the gift of grace and truth. We are not fully empowered when we receive one without the other.

Over the years I have tried to put in a nutshell the "gifts" that good mentors give to mentees. While every mentoring relationship is unique, I believe there are certain universal resources that can be passed on if a mentor wants to invest in someone.

Frequently, I will hear someone say: I have never been in a formal mentoring relationship. What exactly is supposed to transpire when we meet? Is there an optimal format to follow? What sort of exchange should happen between mentor and mentee?

The answer to these questions may vary. There is no one right thing to say or do when you meet with your mentee. I suppose the one common non-negotiable that every good mentor shares is this: they modeled what they taught. *They didn't just say it, they lived it. They practiced what they preached.*

In addition to this essential ingredient, I have listed the God-given resources that I believe every good mentor should impart to their mentee over time. If you are just beginning this process, this list should be especially helpful to you. The following list represents *seven categories* that provide a guideline as you think through what could and should happen on a regular basis.

THE SEVEN GIFTS A MENTOR GIVES

1. ACCOUNTABILITY......This involves holding a person to their commitments to God. It may involve bringing a list of tough questions to the meeting and asking your mentee to respond honestly to them.

2. AFFIRMATION......This involves speaking words of encouragement, love and support to your partner; affirming their strengths, their thoughts, their ministry and their obedience.

3. ASSESSMENT......This involves objectively evaluating their present state and giving them an assessment on what you see; it enables them to gain perspective from an outside point of view.

4. ADVICE......This involves speaking words of wise counsel and giving them options for their decisions. It means providing direction and navigation for their life.

5. ADMONISHMENT......This involves giving them words of caution and warning to enable them to avoid the pitfalls they may not foresee as well as you do. It may mean providing correction.

6. ASSETS......This involves giving them tangible resources, gifts and tools—whether it's a book, a tape, a ministry resource or a personal contact that you can introduce to them.

7. APPLICATION......This involves pointing them in the right direction to find places where they can apply the truth they've learned; it means helping them find a "laboratory" where they can practice.

All of these are gifts, given from the heart and life experience of the mentor. They become especially valuable based on the timing in which they are given. I would suggest that you look for those *teachable moments*, just like parents do with their children—and concentrate on giving these gifts away in those moments. My recommendation is that you memorize this list of "gifts," then be ready to give them away at any time.

Think about it. As you look over the list of gifts again, none of them have to do with possessing an extremely high IQ, lots of talent, or being good looking and famous. *They are gifts that anyone can give away!* As mentors, we will obviously improve with time and experience, but we can all start giving these wonderful gifts to hungry mentees now. The world awaits the treasure you have to offer!

WHAT ARE THE QUALITIES OF AN INFLUENTIAL MENTOR?

Sociologists tell us that the most introverted of persons will influence an average of 10,000 other people during his lifetime. That is a remarkable statistic to me.

If introverted, withdrawn, non-leadership-type individuals influence that many other people, imagine what kind of influence you and I who aspire to leadership might exercise! Influence is what leadership is all about. Remember, it's the simplest one-word definition of leadership. In this chapter, we will discuss how we can effectively influence a mentee through the development of specific character qualities inside us.

WE MUST BE COMMITTED

At the onset, we must make a decision to be committed people—committed to become true mentors. Several years ago I made a specific determination (during my time alone with God) that I was going to mentor willing individuals for the rest of my life. That is who I have become. Commitment is what boosts us over the edge.

I heard a humorous illustration about a kamakazi pilot who was still alive after flying fifty missions! Something was wrong with this picture! A reporter interviewed him after his discharge from the military and asked, "How can you call yourself a kamakazi pilot, yet still be alive after so many flights?" "Well, it's like this," the pilot responded with a grin, "I had a whole lot of involvement. Not much commitment—but a whole lot of involvement."

Sometimes I believe that sounds like us, as Christians. We sample a variety of Christian activities, but often fail to be committed to one that counts. We possess a "tourist" mindset when it comes to our faith.

As we consider the commitment of a mentor, we must reckon that this big commitment must be viewed from three angles:

1. WE MUST BE COMMITTED TO A PERSON.
   Our mentees must sense our commitment to them as people. Not projects. Not duties! We must love *them* and have their best interests in mind. We must be loyal.

2. WE MUST BE COMMITTED TO A PROCESS.
   There will be ups and downs through the season we meet with our mentees. We must step back and see the process they are in and the steps required, understanding the big picture of their lives. We must be discerning.

3. WE MUST BE COMMITTED TO A PURPOSE.
   Our final commitment must be to the end result. We must determine that we will see them from Point "A" to Point "B," or the goal that has been mutually set. In the same way that God will complete the work He has begun in us (Phil. 1:6), we must see the finished product

inside our mentees and fulfill our commitment to them. We must be diligent.

We should not blindly move forward into mentoring without first settling these issues. They represent fundamental commitments that provide a foundation for a healthy relationship. I suggest you carefully pray through each one of them prior to a mentorship.

DEVELOPING THE RIGHT QUALITIES

I suppose the list of character qualities that mentors *ought* to possess could be endless. Further, if I were to simply list every ingredient that goes into the recipe for a great mentor, it would be overwhelming. That would not help us here. However, the following six words provide a guideline that is, indeed, helpful. These six terms represent major categories for you to pray about and pursue as strengths in your life as a leader and mentor. Study and memorize these words that all begin with the letter "I," and make this your "I CAN DO IT" list!

QUALITIES OF A GOOD MENTOR:

1. **INITIATIVE**
   - I give direction in my relationship with my mentee/ sphere of influence.
   - I take responsibility for the health of the relationship.
   - I initiate spiritual dialogue with vulnerability and humility.

2. **INTIMACY**
   - I experience intimacy with God through personal worship and study time.

- I experience intimacy with my mentee through open and honest conversation.

3. INFLUENCE
- I exercise *Biblical influence in my relationship* with my mentee.
- I develop, encourage and facilitate growth in my mentee.
- I am a "giver," a generous contributor in relationships.

4. INTEGRITY
- I lead a life of integrity—honesty that is above reproach.
- I am not ashamed of my "private" world, of what I am when no one is looking.

5. IDENTITY
- I am secure in who I am in Christ.
- I have a healthy, biblical self-image that prevents a defensive attitude.
- I have developed a mature statement of purpose for my life.

6. INNER CHARACTER
- I exhibit the fruit of the Spirit in my life, including self-discipline.
- I am a Spirit-filled, Spirit-led believer.
- I maintain control by submission to God's sovereignty and human authority.

COMMANDMENTS AND COMPONENTS

In the remaining pages of this chapter I'd like to share with you what I have gleaned from men far wiser than I am. John C. Crosby and Dr. Bobby Clinton have both formed checklists of components that make a good mentoring experience. Each provides a sort of "dos and don'ts" advisory that I think is worth including here. Let's begin with Crosby's shorter list.

THE TEN COMMANDMENTS OF MENTORING

1. Thou shalt not play God.
2. Thou shalt not play Teacher.
3. Thou shalt not play Mother or Father.
4. Thou shalt not lie with your body.
5. Active listening is the holy time and thou shalt practice it at every session.
6. Thou shalt be nonjudgmental.
7. Thou shalt not lose heart because of repeated disappointments.
8. Thou shalt practice empathy, not sympathy.
9. Thou shalt not believe that thou can move mountains.
10. Thou shalt not envy thy neighbor's protege, nor thy neighbor's success.

John C. Crosby
The Uncommon Individual Foundation

Bobby Clinton, along with Paul Stanley, created his own Ten Commandments of mentoring in their wonderful book entitled: *Connecting*. This list is actually the essential components that create a positive experience and mentoring relationship. It's a bit more lengthy than the above list, and I have modified it slightly for our purposes here. I'm sure, however, you will benefit from studying it and implementing their suggestions.

COMMANDMENT 1: RELATIONSHIP

The stronger the relationship, the greater the empowerment. Sometimes mentoring relationships just happen and develop in a natural way. Others take time and are more deliberate. Compatibility and chemistry are true advantages, especially for co-mentoring. Some relationships will not grow to an intimate level, and not all need to. But it is important to keep in mind that you need to continue to develop the relationship.

COMMANDMENT 2: PURPOSE

Sometimes mentoring proves disappointing. This disappointment can frequently be traced back to differing or unfulfilled expectations. We find that expectations should be expressed, negotiated, and agreed upon at the beginning of a mentoring relationship. Commandments two through eight all deal with important areas of expectations. Along with expectations, you need to discuss and mutually affirm the purpose or basic aims of the mentoring relationship.

COMMANDMENT 3: REGULARITY

Disappointments can arise from differing expectations as to regularity of meetings between the mentor and the mentee. Some mentors may have in mind less frequent times together, while growing mentees may envision more time together. It is better to talk this over and set some ground rules both for regular meeting times and for impromptu interactions. Availability for impromptu times always facilitates the development of the relationship, but there could be conflict with competing time demands if the mentor is heavily engaged in other priorities. Clarify these issues early on in the relationship.

Intensive mentoring probably works best with at least once-a-week contact either face-to-face or by phone. Regularity may vary if the mentee is a self-starter or a person with heavy responsibilities.

COMMANDMENT 4: ACCOUNTABILITY

Accountability or mutual responsibility is an important mentoring dynamic. Again, it usually does not just happen. You must plan for it. Agree together on how you will establish and monitor mentoring tasks. The heart of empowerment lies not only in what the mentor shares with the mentee, but also in the tasks the mentor gives to the mentee. You must complete the tasks in order to benefit. Accountability is the prod to make sure this happens, because change is difficult and rarely takes place without it. It can occur many ways: written reports, scheduled phone calls, probing questions during meetings, or a planned evaluation time. What a mentor likes to see is a mentee who takes responsibility to see that accountability takes place. The mentee's self-initiative in accountability speeds and enhances empowerment.

COMMANDMENT 5: COMMUNICATION MECHANISMS

Frequently mentors see something in a mentee that needs correction or about which they feel concern. How and when to communicate this is important to clarify early in a mentor relationship. This is particularly important among peers, who are more apt to hold one another accountable in personal areas. As a mentor, I have always asked my mentees, "If I see or learn of an area of need or concern for you—and it may be negative—how and when do you want me to communicate it to you?" It is important to discover timing and procedure so that when the opportunity comes for correction and challenge (and it will!), you are ready for it and can anticipate a mature response. When peers commit to each other, this is important for them to discuss when they make a covenant. A mentee can also initiate this as he or she is in a place to learn, grow, and respond to challenge by the mentor.

COMMANDMENT 6: CONFIDENTIALITY

Commandments five and six have to do with communication. Five concerns communication between mentor and mentee, and six concerns communication *outside* the mentoring relationship. The mentoring relationship, if it deepens, may involve a sharing of personal matters between mentor and mentee. It may be that one or both of them do not want these things conveyed to those outside the relationship.

Several factors influence the level of confidentiality. One factor involves the personalities of both mentor and mentee. Some people are more vulnerable, and others are less vulnerable. Some are not concerned that others know the deep issues of their lives, while others feel threatened by the thought that some may find out about their personal concerns. They may not even want their age known.

A mentoring relationship must honor the participants' personalities and feelings about confidentiality. You will have to explore this with each individual mentoring relationship you set up. In counseling, you should consider all things confidential and not to be shared with others without permission. For other mentoring relationships, you both need to make it clear when something you share should be treated as confidential. Such a simple statement to each other will free you to speak openly and may save much grief later on.

COMMANDMENT 7: LIFE CYCLES OF MENTORING

Periods of mentoring vary in length of time for empowerment to happen. You should realize this and set reasonable time lengths for the type of mentoring you are involved in. *Avoid open-ended relationships.* When you enter a mentoring relationship, do not expect it to last forever. In fact, we prefer breaking up potentially long mentoring experiences into obvious or logical segments, so that at each juncture closure can be made if desired. If you assume that the given purposes and accountability measures will take six months, set up a smaller goal of three months with evaluation. Then both of you can back out without losing face if the mentoring relationship does not meet your expectations. On the other hand, if it goes well you can continue the relationship and set up a new evaluation point. Better to have short periods, evaluation, and closure points with the possibility of reentry than have a sour relationship for a long time that each fears terminating.

In summary, here are the basic guidelines: Set realistic time limits. Have exit points where both parties can leave without bad relations. Have open doors where the invitation to continue can be open. Recognize the necessity of a time limit in any mentoring situation.

COMMANDMENT 8: EVALUATION

No mentoring relationship is ideal. Expectations are seldom totally realized. From time to time the mentoring relationship should be evaluated. Wise mentors will use the three dynamic factors (attraction, responsiveness, accountability) and empowerment to help them evaluate the ongoing state of the mentoring venture. This allows for mid-course corrections. Evaluation is dominantly a mentor function. Mentees will sense growth but will not have the perspective to effectively evaluate; therefore, a joint evaluation is best.

In fact, in preparing for mentoring sessions it is a good idea for the mentor to review the whole process and see where progress has been made, where there are problems, and what should be done at the present juncture to improve the mentoring.

The following is an example of the evaluation steps I suggest you take as a mentor:

Step 1: Mentor evaluates first, on his own.
- Lacks attention
- Little prayer
- Assignments not really on target
- Interest is flagging
- Ready to go on
- Need to redefine

Step 2: Mentor initiates appropriate self-correction.

Step 3: Evaluate and discuss—mentor and mentee.

Step 4: Mutual agreement to redefine or modify expectations.

COMMANDMENT 9: EXPECTATIONS

Commandments eight and nine are two sides of the same coin. While evaluation (commandment eight) is mainly the responsibility of the mentor, expectation, commandment nine, is mainly the responsibility of the mentee.

Expectations are the root of most disappointing mentoring experiences. The basic rule that can offset missed expectations is a simple one: Use evaluation and feedback to modify your expectations so that they fit your real-life mentoring situation. Recognize that you will seldom reach ideal expectations, because real-life situations have complexities you cannot always anticipate. After a time of mentoring, modify what you ideally hoped for down to what is most likely going to happen. Recognize that there will be empowerment and rejoice in that. Lack of meeting ideal expectations does not have to be the source of dissatisfaction in mentoring.

COMMANDMENT 10: CLOSURE

A basic rule in planning that is being passed around more and more is, "Begin with the end in mind." All mentoring should follow this basic notion. Closure has to do with bringing a satisfactory end to a mentoring experience. Vertical mentoring that has no clear end in mind will usually dwindle to nothing with uneasy feelings on the part of both people. Vertical mentoring is not intended to be an ongoing experience. A happy ending for a mentoring experience involves closure in which both parties evaluate, recognize how and where empowerment has occurred, and mutually end the mentoring relationship. What frequently happens in successfully closed mentoring is an ongoing friendship that allows for occasional mentoring and future interweaving of lives as needed. So then, don't forget this final commandment:

"Bring closure to the mentoring relationship." This is probably the most violated of all of the commandments, and the most detrimental. Even unsuccessful mentoring experiences should have closure.

WHAT CAN I DO TO BE A SUCCESSFUL MENTOR?

It was a Romanian pastor who first spoke these profound words to me:

"Success. . .without a successor. . .is a failure."

Read that again. That one phrase captures the heartbeat of mentoring. Each of us who mentor want to do it well. We want to see our mentees take what we've given them and flourish with it. They are, in many ways, the next generation—the "successors" that will follow us in life. If we didn't believe in building successors, we probably wouldn't be mentoring. This chapter concerns itself with enabling you to mentor well. I hope to put some fundamental tools in your toolbox that will help you do it successfully.

Bobb Biehl, head of Masterplanning Group, International, shares these paraphrased thoughts about the core of successful mentoring.

When people hear the word *mentor*, they tend to think of a white-haired person who is old and feeble, and/or rich and famous. And when they hear the word *protege*, they tend to think of a kid on a piano bench learning the keyboard from the maestro.

But in reality, the mentor-protege relationship in its simplest form is a lot like a big brother, big sister relationship. The big brother really wants to see the little brother win. It isn't that the mentor has to be older. But he or she must want very badly to see another person win, and be committed to helping them win.

In my devotional book, *The Greatest Mentors in the Bible*, I illustrate this beautiful truth. One of my favorite portraits of a mentor went on display before the entire world at the 1992 Summer Olympics in Barcelona, Spain. Derrick Redman, an athlete from England, had qualified to compete in the 440 meter event despite the fact that he'd had 22 surgeries on his Achilles heel. It was a miracle to some that he was even able to run again, not to mention qualifying for the Olympics.

It was at the event, however, that tragedy struck. Midway through the race Derrick Redman pulled up short and fell to the ground. He had pulled a hamstring and faced still another injury. At least one of the cameras stayed glued to this athlete as he got up and limped forward, wincing in pain. He could barely stay on his feet. His hopes of winning were dashed, and while he wanted desperately to finish the race, even this looked impossible. Derrick wept as he realized it was all over for him.

Enter his mentor. Sitting in the stands, second row from the top, was Jim Redman, Derrick's father. He could not imagine doing anything else but getting involved. He pushed his way past the huge crowd separating him from the track. He persistently moved toward the gate and pushed through the security guards. They would not keep this man from his mentee. Jim had been Derrick's biggest fan through the years, and this move was the only logical one for him. The cameras quickly focused on this intruder running toward the pitiful athlete from the UK. Jim put his arm around his son and the two exchanged words. In tears,

Derrick fell into his father's arms, and then Jim did what all great mentors do for their mentees. Jim lifted Derrick up, put his son's arm over his own shoulder, and the two finished the race together.

I remember watching this scene with tears in my eyes. I had not expected to observe such an act of love that day—to receive such a clear snapshot of someone investing in the life of another. I can remember the crowd applauding for the two of them as they finished the race arm in arm, as loudly as they did the winner of the race that day. Whether he knew it or not, Jim Redman gave the world a picture of a mentor: one who picks up the life of another and says, "I'm going to help you finish your race well."

THE DIFFERENT KINDS OF MENTORS

If you are not mentoring now, it may be because you don't feel you have what it takes to be a mentor. In other words, you possess an unrealistic stereotype of a wise, elderly "Moses figure" that has lots of time and talent to disciple young proteges. Like so many others, you may feel you have neither the time nor the talent to give. If so, let me liberate you. You actually *can* mentor others well, but you may have to change your mental image of a mentor.

In their insightful book, *Connecting,* Dr. Robert Clinton and Paul Stanley outline the seven different kinds of mentors that most often exist in our lives. It is important for us to examine these seven roles for two reasons:

1. To determine which kind we most need in our own life

2. To determine which kind we are best suited to be for someone else

Knowing your personal style and gifts will enable you to better decide what kind of mentor you need for yourself right now at this season in your life, and what role you will successfully fulfill in a mentee's life. Note these seven kinds of mentors below:

1. DISCIPLER
Helping with the basics of following Christ

2. SPIRITUAL GUIDE
Accountability, direction/insight for maturation

3. COACH
Motivation, skills needed to meet a task/challenge

4. COUNSELOR
Timely advice, perspective on self, others, ministry

5. TEACHER
Knowledge, understanding on a specific subject

6. SPONSOR
Career guidance, protection; network with contacts

7. MODEL
A living personal example for life, ministry, career

You will observe that each of these roles provides a different kind of service to someone. Some are best suited for close, regular inspections of the spiritual life of the mentee. The discipler, for example, is needed most in a mentee's early days as a Christian. Frequency of meetings and strict enforcement of accountability are more essential during those days than for a spiritually mature mentee. Later in our spiritual lives we may not need the same kind of questions to be asked of us by our mentor. In fact, the mentor we need at that point is very different. As a mature person, we need more of a consultant—meetings are less frequent, but the issues are deeper. The bottom line is: *we need different kinds of mentors at different stages of life.*

This table of various mentor roles is helpful and liberating. First, because it prevents us from an unrealistic pursuit of one ideal mentor—or a pursuit to become an ideal, perfect mentor. Second, it can help all of us see which role we are best suited to play. I, for one, am much better suited to meet with mature mentees who may be preparing for ministry than with new Christians working through the details of their early Christian life. I have done both, and I am more fulfilled at playing the former role; it fits my style and gifts far better. Third, the list of seven roles serves as a guide for us in the different seasons of our lives. Right now I do not need a discipler as much as I need a coach and a sponsor. All of this should spark us to seek these key relationships.

A lot of men and women are successful managers. They've managed well their own company, a church, or another type of organization. And good management is what brings that feeling of success. Then deep down inside they begin to think, *I wonder who I could develop and bring along as a protege.*

Mal King, in the manuscript for his book *Mentoring, the Only Way To Develop Leaders,* paraphrases Ashley Montagu's definition of love as it applies to mentoring:

"Mentoring is the demonstrated, active involvement in the welfare of another in such a way that one not only contributes to the survival of the other, but does so in a creatively enlarging manner, in a manner calculated to stimulate the potentialities of the other so that they may develop to their optimum capacity. It is to communicate to the other that one is profoundly interested in him, that one is there to offer him all the supports and stimulations he requires for the realization of his potentialities for being a person able to relate himself to others in a creatively enlarging manner, who gives the psychological support and sustenance the other requires, to nourish and to enable him to grow not only in his potentialities for being a harmonic being but also to train him in the development of those inner controls that will make external ones unnecessary."

Wow! What a snapshot of a mentor. Clearly, Bobb Biehl and Mal King give us at least a blueprint from which to operate. Our work is cut out for us. But before we itemize the details of what makes a successful mentor, let's briefly examine the pitfalls we must avoid. In the same way that we all hold incredible potential for developing people successfully, we all hold the opportunity to damage them as well. Authority can be abused; ignorance can prevent us from doing what we ought; lack of discernment may cause us to say something hurtful or mistaken. The following list was first developed by Richard H. Tyre for The Uncommon Individual Foundation. He calls it:

HOW TO SPOT A TOXIC MENTOR

1. **The Avoider**

   "Of course we'll get together, but I'm too busy today."

   Initial enthusiasm but later inaccessibility. Not available when the need is greatest. Cannot get close emotionally. Unintentionally forgets to share organizational information or helpful personal affirmation.

2. **The Dumper**

   "A protege? I'd love a dedicated assistant!"

Opposite to the Avoider. Is delighted to give the mentee opportunities, assignments, extra work, more responsibility, but gives inadequate guidance; the mentee is abandoned. All that is given is work.

3. **The Criticizer**
   "Let me take this opportunity to show you why that's not the right way to do it."

   Believes mentoring is a license to point out mistakes. Gives the mentee responsibility—maybe too much, too soon—and then criticizes them for inexperience and poor performance. Unconsciously keeps them subordinate.

4. **The User**
   "My wife doesn't understand me. You're not breaking up anything; we were already pretty far apart."

   The mentee is the mentor's spy in the ranks. They run up the flags. They are a convenient, pleasant companion, backboard or source of ideas. They are used for the mentor's benefit.

5. **The Black Halo**
   You have the perfect mentor. Unfortunately, anyone associated with that person becomes poison in the organizaton.

   The mentor teaches the mentee all there is to know, but policy has changed, and his way of operating is out of favor.

6. **The Queen Bee**
   "I made it in a much tougher time by myself. You can, too."

Doesn't believe that the mentee should show a need for help. The Attrition Theory: "I made it by hard work, brains and luck, but they made it by knowing someone!" The mentee feels inferior.

WHAT IS A SUCCESSFUL MENTOR, ANYWAY?

In our context a successful mentor is one who assumes responsibility for the *development* of his mentee. The key term is "development." The successful mentor is going to be a:

♦ Guide
♦ Encourager
♦ Resource
♦ Evaluator
♦ Provider

When I think of the term "mentor," it conjures up images of a tradesman or craftsman developing a young apprentice in old England. Can you see it? Cobblestone streets with horses and carriages, a shop off the main street where this craftsman works—all the while being observed by an up-and-coming young man who wants one day to own a shop of his own. The craftsman spends time explaining his work to the curious, onlooking apprentice, allowing him to try his hand at doing the work himself to gain the skill, then debriefing the young man at the close of the day. What a beautiful analogy for the spiritual mentor.

Dr. Tony Campolo, in his book *Who Switched the Price Tags?,* reports the results of a survey of retired people living in their twilight years. In response to the question, "If you could live your life over again, what changes would you make?" they shared three common answers:

♦ I would reflect more. (I would take the time to stop and

make sense of the journey I was on.)

♦ I would risk more. (I played it too safe. I would take more risks in the areas that count.)

♦ I would invest my life in areas that will outlive me. (I would try to leave a legacy by investing in the lives of others.)

All three answers are insightful, but note the third one again. That statement is the vision and fruit of a mentor. It is pouring your life, wisdom, skills and spirit into the life of another so that there is spiritual reproduction—life multiplication. Does this sound strangely biblical? If Jesus called us to "make disciples of all nations," might that best begin with those already in our sphere of influence? Mentoring is the ultimate in spiritual leadership. It is making disciples.

I cannot think of a wiser investment of our time and energy than in the people God has placed right under our noses. They are eternal treasures, immortal souls with the potential of Jesus within them (John 14:12, I John 2:6). I believe we were designed for that kind of fulfilling, satisfying investment. A television interview reminded me of this some years ago. Just after the annual Rose Bowl Parade in Pasadena, California, a young float builder was interviewed and asked whether he enjoyed constructing those huge, multifaceted floats each year. When he replied that he did, he was asked if he had considered doing it as a career. His response was a decisive "No," and then he explained why: "I could never imagine investing so much of myself into something that's thrown into the scrap pile within a matter of weeks." Great insight! How often do we sell ourselves short by investing so much in insignificant, temporal and trivial causes?

In the first part of this century a young boy was scarred for life by his parents as he grew up during World War I in Germany. His family, the Schicklewubers, had developed distorted priorities that left the boy emotionally alone and confused. He overheard his father talk about moving away one evening, and assumed that he would be abandoned. He decided then to toughen up and find refuge in things outside of love and family. The world has suffered much from that decision; for you and I know this young boy as Nazi dictator Adolf Hitler. I have to wonder how history might have been altered if young Adolf had had a godly mentor available to him.

SOME PRACTICAL SUGGESTIONS

I trust you are convinced that our world needs mentors, good mentors who want to successfully make deposits in the lives of their mentees. Let's close this chapter by getting very practical. The following "to do" lists are functions you can perform right now to become a more effective mentor.

IF YOU ARE A TEACHER. . .you have probably given some good thought to the subject of mentoring. But don't mistake the two. Teaching (in North America, anyway) expects the student to remain relatively passive in the learning process. We've embraced the Greek model of education which is academic and informational. The Hebrew model (which Jesus employed) is based much more on relationship and experience, and is transformational. Mentoring, as we have discussed already, demands relationship, conversation and some degree of shared experience. Teachers can, however, become great mentors. Here are some suggestions about becoming a teacher who mentors effectively. These were modified from a list by Bobby Clinton:

1. Catalog the major subjects you can teach so you are

     ready to share them.

2. Recognize how you would tailor them to work with an individual.

3. Make it known that you have resources available to help others in the areas of your knowledge.

4. Be sure to model or demonstrate the principles you are sharing.

5. As you teach to impart knowledge, illustrate also the dynamics of the teaching/learning process. This motivates learners and suggests to them how and why they, too, can use the knowledge with others.

6. Revise the knowledge base to fit your mentee's situation. Do not overkill. Teach what is needed.

7. Challenge your mentee to use it. You do this best by demonstrating its usefulness in your own life and by showing relevancy to the mentee's situation.

8. If you teach in a group context, be on the lookout for those who should be mentored individually. You may want to invite those who respond well into a special relationship that will allow them to move more rapidly.

9. Be open to unique teaching sessions where needed. When requests come for teaching that do not fit your normal patterns, think of the possibility of empowerment for the individuals concerned. That is, be open to mentoring via teaching.

Teachers who are open to deliberate mentoring and establishing personal relationships with people in order to empower them through teaching are greatly needed. Perhaps God is challenging you toward this important kind of mentoring.

IF YOU ARE A COUNSELOR. . .you are very often already assuming the role of a mentor with your clients. After all, therapy is speaking into the life of the counselee. The difference, however, lies in the fact that counseling is often reactive instead of proactive. It is reacting or responding to an unhealthy emotional state in someone, and therapy ends when balance comes again. Mentoring, however, should not come to closure (ideally) until the mentee is actively pursuing their role as a contributor to their world—seeking someone that they might mentor.

Since both a counselor and a mentor are guides for others, this is a good, definitive word to embrace as a role. Most people need personal guidance on spiritual issues throughout their lifetime. As a counselor, you can become an effective mentor/guide if you'll consistently perform these functions:

♦ Help believers assess their own development.
♦ Point out areas of strength and weakness in spirituality.
♦ Help believers identify needs and take initiative for change and growth.
♦ Provide perspectives on how to develop growth and depth.
♦ Provide accountability for spiritual maturity.

IF YOU SIMPLY WANT TO IMPROVE YOUR MENTORING SKILLS...then I would suggest you consistantly do the following list. As you do, you will increase your impact and deepen your spiritual leadership in the life of the mentee.

1. **Invest time and energy in this.** Spend some time discussing this concept of mentoring with your mentee. Have them share their perceptions of their strengths, weaknesses, and openness to this process.

2. **Know yourself.** If you're going to help others in their growth, you must know your own strengths, weak-

nesses, and personality traits. Good mentors always do.

3. **Cultivate generosity.** Good mentors have learned to be givers in relationships and realize that it is more blessed (and natural) to give then receive.

4. **Study leadership.** Read books and talk with people who can teach you how to be a better leader. You need to understand leadership issues. Good mentors always have mentors.

5. **Initiate vulnerability.** If you want an intimate, transparent, teachable mentee, start practicing those qualities yourself. This accelerates the growth process.

6. **Model character.** If you want to pass on a trait or skill, remember: First you do it, then you do it as the mentee observes; then he does it as you observe; then he does it—whether you're there or not.

7. **Pray for vision.** Ask God to help you see His purposes for your mentee. This will help you really believe in them. Ask Him to build in you the following qualities of a good mentor:

   ◆ Patience with people (Long-suffering)
   ◆ Ability to see the big picture (Vision)
   ◆ Commitment to relationships (Accountability)
   ◆ Enjoyment in giving (Generosity)
   ◆ Strong personal discipline (Character)
   ◆ Good communication (Communicative)
   ◆ Understanding of others (Discernment)

SOMEONE OUT THERE NEEDS YOU!

I believe there is a potential "giant" somewhere out there who needs you to become their mentor. Despite your feelings of inadequacy, you need to take a step and go after them. A journey of a thousand miles begins with a single step. Sure, you will run into conflict and hardship; you may likely find a young mentee who says he or she wants to be challenged—then promptly runs from it! Go after them. Whether they know it or not, they need you.

Let me close with this analogy. Driving along a freeway one night, a woman noticed the headlights of a huge semi-truck tailgating her much too closely. She sped up, but so did the truck. She became afraid and drove even faster. Finally she exited the freeway and raced toward a nearby gas station. The truck followed her in. She leaped from her car and ran into the garage as onlookers stood by. The truck driver then climbed down from his cab, walked to her car and pulled a would-be rapist from her back seat! The trucker had spotted the man from his higher vantage point and had determined to save the woman from harm. The woman, in essence, was running from the wrong man.

In a similar way, a mentee may run from or resist the help of a mentor because of different vantage points and a misunderstanding of motives. And too often we give up our attempts to mentor because helping them is just too much of a hassle.

Trust me—there is a hassle to the business of mentoring. There are risks, as well. That's why so few do it. But remember: to get to the fruit, you've got to go out on a limb.

How Do I Confront Effectively?

This chapter deals with the least popular part of mentoring: confrontation. No healthy, balanced person actually enjoys the act of confronting someone over a sin, attitude, omission, gossip, disobedience or failure to follow-through. Those kinds of meetings always seem to cause our stomachs to churn, our hands and heads to sweat, and our wills to weaken. We can and should learn to love the fruit of such interaction, but only a sadistic person enjoys doing the confronting!

Even the word "confront" is a heavy word. It seems so demeaning, so warlike. I believe we ought to make an adjustment right off the bat if we're going to engage in confrontation effectively. Dr. John Maxwell suggests that we should use the word "clarification" more often than "confrontation." It paints a more relational picture. Most of the time, when there is a problem, we are merely clarifying a misunderstanding or miscommunication anyway. When we approach our mentee with the attitude that we simply want to clarify rather than indict them or punish them for their obvious failure, we are able to maintain a much more loving and compassionate demeanor. Good advice.

LAYING A FOUNDATION

When our mentee has done an apparent wrong, and we believe it is significant enough to discuss it with them, we need to operate from a biblical foundation. If you are wavering on whether or not the Bible is clear on the subject, review the following passages:

1) **2 Corinthians 10:4-5** - The tools of our trade are divinely powerful to challenge people's thinking.

2) **1 Thessalonians 5:14** - Remind, warn, admonish, and encourage the fainthearted.

3) **2 Timothy 3:16** - Scripture is profitable for teaching, reproof, correction, and training.

4) **2 Timothy 4:2-4** - Preach, reprove, rebuke, and exhort.

5) **Colossians 1:28** - Admonish (warn by reminding) people.

6) **Titus 1:13** - Reprove severely that they may be sound in faith.

In addition, keep the following statements in mind, as you consider the discussion with your mentee. These statements represent the bottom line or the objectives you'll want to embrace in your meeting. These are why you must confront when appropriate.

- ◆ You want to see them transformed by the power of God.
- ◆ The goal is not condemnation, but restoration.

♦ Challenging them to grow must go beyond good advice.
♦ People need help with the practical application of scriptural truth.
♦ We must love truth more than anything else in this world.

Kent Amos, former Xerox executive and now head of the Washington based Urban Family Institute, said recently:

"We never think of helping troubled young people to change their lives by giving them the guidance and education and training they need. Instead, we think punitively: Three strikes and you're out, two years and you're off welfare—even if you have no place else to go."

In many ways, he's right. It's time we become proactive with our attention toward this generation. It's time we "built a fence at the top of the cliff rather than a hospital at the bottom." The only way we can succeed in this preventative way is to confront issues before it's too late.

STEPS TOWARD EFFECTIVE CONFRONTATION

I have lost count of the number of occasions where I have had to confront a person I was mentoring or discipling. I would often try to talk myself out of doing it, thinking that if I just ignored the problem it would go away. That, of course, is rarely true. I have never regretted confronting a situation when I did it biblically. In fact, at this point in my life I believe successful confrontation was the most important lesson I learned as a pastor.

The following list represents the steps I generally take when confronting a mentee. Keep in mind that confrontation (or clarification) is right only when the issue is clear and biblical (i.e., the mentee has violated scripture or not kept a commitment/agreement you've both agreed upon). When this is the case, walk though this process.

1. **PRAY THROUGH YOUR ANGER.**
   Don't let emotion lead you. Wait until you're objective, but try to deal with issues before they become big ones.

2. **YOU INITIATE THE CONTACT.**
   Don't wait for them to initiate. Scripture beckons you to make things right whether you're the offender or the offended.

3. **BEGIN WITH AFFIRMATION.**
   Speak words of love and encouragement first. Then receive fresh permission to challenge them.

4. **TELL THEM *YOU* HAVE A PROBLEM OR STRUGGLE.**
   Don't say it's their problem, but yours; own the fact that you have wrestled with this issue.

5. **AS YOU BRING UP THE ISSUE, EXPLAIN THAT YOU DON'T UNDERSTAND WHY THIS IS. . .**
   Aim to clarify. Always give them the benefit of the doubt. Believe the best and allow them to explain themselves. When you speak, however, be loving and clear.

6. **ESTABLISH FORGIVENESS AND REPENTANCE.**
   Connect the issue you are correcting with who they are in Christ. Don't conclude the meeting until forgiveness is extended and issues resolved.

7. **COMPROMISE ON OPINIONS, NOT ON CONVICTIONS OR PRINCIPLES.**
   Determine what you will die for. Be flexible with your opinions, but not on biblical principles.

8. **PRAY AND AFFIRM YOUR LOVE AT THE END.**
   Always close these times with prayer. Give them hope and a future through your words.

An unexamined life, said Socrates, is not worth living. A mentor's wounds are those of a faithful friend. Not everyone has the right to climb into a mentee's life and offer rebuke. It must be the mentor who has built a love relationship beforehand. Alfred Whitehead once said, "Apart from blunt truth, our lives sink decadently amid the perfume of hints and suggestions."

Chuck Swindoll tells the story of a lady who made an appointment with a pastor to talk about joining his church. She said the surgeon who had performed her face lift told her, "My dear, I have done an extraordinary job on your face, as you can see in the mirror. I have charged you a great deal of money and you were happy to pay it. But I want to give you some free advice. Find a group of people who love God and who will love you enough to help you deal with all of the negative emotions inside of you. If you don't, you'll be back in my office in a short time with your face in far worse shape than before."

YOUR ATTITUDE

Very likely, the attitude you have when you are confronting/clarifying will be more important than the words you speak. Do your best to embrace these additional principles when meeting with your mentee:

- ◆ BE GENEROUS (Both words and actions)
- ◆ BELIEVE IN PEOPLE
- ◆ STAY LOYAL
- ◆ TAKE A STAND
- ◆ BE EXCITED ABOUT ANY IMPROVEMENT
- ◆ AFFIRM PEOPLE

Affirming your belief in your mentee is never more crucial than when you are confronting/clarifying a tough issue in their life. They must know, beyond a shadow of a doubt, that you believe in them. Dale Carnegie illustrates this need with the following story.

In the early 19th century, a young man in London aspired to be a writer. But everything seemed to be against him. He had never been able to attend school more than four years. His father had been thrown in jail because he couldn't pay his debts, and this young man often knew the pangs of hunger. Finally he got a job pasting labels on bottles in a rat-infested warehouse, and he slept at night in a dismal attic room with two other boys—guttersnipes from the slums of London. He had so little confidence in his ability to write that he sneaked out and mailed his first manuscript in the dead of the night so nobody would laugh at him. Story after story was refused. Finally the great day came when one was accepted. True, he wasn't paid for it, but one editor had praised him. One editor had given him recognition. He was so thrilled that he wandered about aimlessly around the streets with tears rolling down his cheeks.

The praise, the recognition that he received through getting one story in print changed his whole life. If it hadn't been for that encouragement, he might have spent his entire life working in rat-infested factories. You may have heard of that boy. His name is Charles Dickens.

THE APPLICATION OF ACCOUNTABILITY

The term "accountability" has become another popular word in the day we live. It has been defined in a number of elaborate ways. My favorite definition for it is simply helping people keep their commitments to God. Period. I suggest you and your mentee discuss the five toughest areas of obedience for each of you at the beginning of your relationship. (These may include lust, lack of discipline, not sticking to a budget, thought life, gossip, etc.) Then exchange your lists and invite each other to ask about those areas on a regular basis. Always close the question/answer period with: "Have you been completely honest with your responses?"

Let me close this chapter by posing some personal questions of my own to you.

Is someone accountable to you so that you can make them accountable to God? Can you name one or more people outside your family to whom you have made yourself accountable? Are you aware of the dangers of unaccountability—dangers such as blind spots, unhealthy relationships, unspoken motives that will never be known without such a friend? When was the last time you gave an account for the private areas of your life to someone outside your family? These would include your finances, occupational diligence or lack of it, your attitude at the office, or packing too many hours of work into each day. How about an appraisal of your friendship? Or your struggles with besetting sins?

As a mentor, develop the courage and the right motive to confront. For the good of the protege and for the good of the Church, "Love must be sincere. Hate what is evil; cling to what is good. Be devoted to one another in brotherly love. Honor one another above yourselves. Never be lacking in zeal, but keep your spiritual fervor, serving the Lord." (Romans 12:9-11)

One word of truth outweighs the world. And one mentor of truth impacts the whole world. That mentor can be you.

HOW DO I SPEAK WITH AUTHORITY INTO SOMEONE'S LIFE?

Sooner or later I suppose every one of us longs to speak with authority when addressing that special "someone" in our life. Parents pray for authority as their children become teenagers and test every boundary in front of them. Coaches long for it as they encounter key players or crucial games during the season. Pastors consistently look for ways to gain authority and influence in the lives of the people in their congregations.

Clearly, this is one of the central issues in the life of a mentor as well. How can I speak into the life of my mentee and be relevant, profound, timely and life transforming? How can I share with them in such a way that it empowers them? How can my words carry weight so that the mentee not only listens to them, but trusts them enough to act on them? How can my wise counsel be appropriately heard as "thus saith the Lord?"

Obviously, not everything we say should carry that much weight. We are human and sometimes hold opinions that are faulty. From time to time, however, we really want to be heard—and ought to be heard—and responded to with great resolve. As mentors, there are times (like it or not) when we speak for God. We are His ambassadors to our mentees. This is a sobering thought. It is a responsible position to be in, and it is our humbling privilege to exercise this role.

The late Dr. Nathaniel Bowditch was a captain who led a number of ocean voyages through dangerous waters. As early as age 21, he sailed an East Indian voyage and began to feel the weight of mentoring the young sailors on board with him. He knew most of them would be nothing but sailors all their lives unless someone began to invest in them, and train them to go beyond their job descriptions. He painstakingly began to instruct the entire crew of the ship in the art of navigation. He shared all he knew with those rugged seamen despite the expense of time and sleep. The results were extraordinary. Without exception, every sailor on board during that voyage later became the captain of a ship. Needless to say, that's a rare occurrence. But such are the natural consequences of associating with a man who senses the responsibility of making deposits in others, and whose generosity earns a position of authority in everyone he contacts.

"Speaking into the life" of your mentee is a learned art. Speaking with authority is an earned right. Both what you learn and earn can increase your influence with them. Let's take a look at both of these components.

SPEAKING INTO THEIR LIFE

I love the term "speaking into their life." It implies that we are speaking personally and intimately to them. It also implies that we are speaking words of direction or perspective that will impact them.

The first evidence we see of this practice in the Bible is when Old Testament patriarchs would bless their sons. Back then it was common for fathers to speak words of blessing (affirmation and direction) to their children as they grew into adulthood. It was a "rite of passage" for young men. We read in Genesis about Jacob blessing his sons with specific words of affirmation for each of them. It was as though these fathers knew the intrinsic need we all have for someone in authority to believe in us and tell us so. Authors Gary Smalley and John Trent have written an excellent book called *The Blessing*. In it they describe the five elements of this blessing.

THE BLESSING CONSISTS OF...

1. Meaningful Touch
2. Spoken Word
3. Expression of High Value
4. Description of a Special Future (word pictures)
5. Application of Genuine Commitment

We live in an age where people seem more wounded than ever. It is now common to come from a past involving divorce, abuse, dysfunction, addictive behavior or co-dependent relationships. Needy people are everywhere. So, how does this affect our mentoring? Do we simply try to avoid them, ignore them or pretend they aren't there? Obviously, we cannot do this if we intend to lead as Jesus does. Instead, we need to recover this Old Testament practice performed by Hebrew leaders (patriarchs and priests) on their people and families. This practice came to be known as giving the blessing to others.

WHAT'S HAPPENED TO US?

With the Fall of man, Adam lost his security and sense of significance. In one very real sense, he lost his identity, his self-esteem. Hence, we have struggled since, whether we live in America or Romania, with personal needs that often go unmet in a healthy way. Thousands of years ago, young men used to struggle over receiving the blessing—remember Jacob and Esau? I believe people still struggle today. Note the following three components necessary for inner health:

1. *A SENSE OF WORTH.*
   IF MISSING, WE FEEL INFERIOR.

2. *A SENSE OF BELONGING.*
   IF MISSING, WE FEEL INSECURE.

3. *A SENSE OF PURPOSE/COMPETENCE.*
   IF MISSING, WE FEEL INADEQUATE.

SPOTTING THE SYMPTOMS

How do we know when the blessing has not been received by our mentee? There is no scientific formula to answer that question. However, the following symptoms are often clues to the absence of the blessing:

A. HOSTILE SPIRIT

B. UNGRATEFUL SPIRIT

C. INSECURITY

D. INEXPRESSIVE

E. INDEPENDENT SPIRIT

F. DRIVEN SPIRIT

G. TENDENCY TO SABOTAGE SELF

H. CO-DEPENDENCY (Rescuer or needs to be rescued)

People attempt to meet the need for security and significance through many artificial means. You may recognize some of the following:

1. Performance
2. Possessions
3. Pleasure
4. Power
5. People (relationships)

> *The principle: What I view as my source will determine my course.*

It has become my conviction that if a natural authority figure (i.e., parent) has neglected to give the blessing to their child, then God will use mentors to bless them and instill the necessary confidence and competence. Through healthy physical touch and hugs, verbal expressions of affirmation, and casting clear vision for what they could become, mentees can grow far beyond their expectations, and further than what a classroom could ever accomplish.

Notice the diagram on the next page, entitled Exhibit 11-1. I believe it illustrates what every mentor should know about their mentee. It is a graphic of a weed and its root. The weed represents the negative behavior or habit you can see. The root represents the internal conflict (below the surface) you cannot see. The point is—for every weed in our lives, there is a root cause. Usually it involves a person whom we believe has failed us. Going deeper, we often cannot forgive them because we expected them to meet a need in our life. When they cannot meet that need, we feel we cannot forgive them. Ultimately, when you probe deeper, the real issue to resolve is self-worth. This must come from God. We should never place our emotional health in the hands of a person. However, the mentor must bless their mentee until they believe in their God-given self-worth.

Exhibit 11 - 1

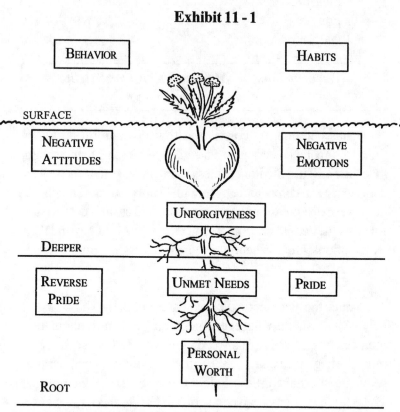

PROGRAMMING→BELIEF→ATTITUDE→FEELINGS→BEHAVIOR→HABITS

SPEAKING WITH AUTHORITY

Now that we've defined what it means to "speak into the life" of someone, let's examine how we can do all of this—with authority. Gaining authority in someone's life doesn't come easily or naturally unless you are their parent; even then it may be difficult! To have authority means to carry influence with a mentee.

Strong leadership equals deep influence.

So, how do we earn deep influence in a mentee's life? Good question. The best way to answer it may be for you to think of the influential people in YOUR past. Perhaps it was a teacher or a parent, a coach or a youth pastor. Can you think of someone? Now ask yourself: How did they gain influence in my life? Your answer may tell you what you must do with your mentee. They likely spent quality time with you; they probably believed in you and really seemed to care about your life. I'm sure they were genuine and encouraging. Most of these ingredients that earn deep influence in a mentee have to do with ATTITUDE, not APTITUDE. They have to do with our heart more than our head, and can be implemented by every one of us today. We do NOT need greater talents, higher IQ or more skills. We must simply decide to do what we know to do.

To summarize, I have taken the word "INFLUENCE" and used each letter to remind you of what good leaders have done to gain influence in the life of individuals. If you'll practice these nine elements, you'll be influential.

HOW TO GAIN INFLUENCE WITH PEOPLE

I - INVESTMENT IN PEOPLE
N - NATURAL WITH PEOPLE
F - FAITH IN PEOPLE
L - LISTENING TO PEOPLE
U - UNDERSTANDING OF PEOPLE
E - ENCOURAGER TO PEOPLE
N - NAVIGATE FOR PEOPLE
C - CONCERN FOR PEOPLE
E - ENTHUSIASM OVER PEOPLE

Let's take a look at what these qualities mean in detail. Remember, each of these qualities have more to do with your heart and your attitude than they do with your gifts and your intelligence. Study them and reflect on how you might apply them.

INVESTMENT IN PEOPLE - Mentors invest in and make deposits in the hearts of people.

NATURAL WITH PEOPLE - Mentors are genuine and don't try to hide their humanity.

FAITH IN PEOPLE - Mentors are optimists and believe in their mentees.

LISTENING TO PEOPLE - Mentors know they earn their right to speak through listening.

UNDERSTANDING OF PEOPLE - Mentors have a keen discernment about what makes people tick.

ENCOURAGER TO PEOPLE - Mentors naturally find the good in others and affirm it.

NAVIGATE FOR PEOPLE - Mentors offer wise words of direction and uncover the best options.

CONCERN FOR PEOPLE - Mentors give love and compassion to others.

ENTHUSIASM OVER PEOPLE - Mentors exhibit a zeal and passion for those they invest in.

INCURABLE OPTIMISM

Let me summarize this chapter by saying that if we're going to be able to speak into the life of our mentee, we must develop an incurable optimism about them and about the future. We must possess a zeal for people and for tomorrow.

Early one morning in a crowded elevator, a businessman became annoyed by another's cheerfulness. "What are you so happy about?" he growled.

"Well, sir, I ain't never lived this day before!" came the reply.

No one else in the elevator had either, but the one who had the optimism and perception to see the possibilities of the new day became, for a brief moment, a mentor to the rest. Such quality of life cannot be taught, only caught.

Frank Lloyd Wright had it. At the age of eighty-three he was asked which of his architectural works he would select as his most important. He replied, "The next one."

Viktor Frankl, who spent years in a Nazi concentration camp, had it. He noticed that those who believed in tomorrow best survived the day. Those who believed that tomorrow would never come were those who did not survive:

> *The prisoner who had lost his faith in the future—his future—was doomed. With his loss of belief in the future, he also lost his spiritual hold; he let himself decline and become subject to mental and physical decay.*

Anne Mansfield Sullivan had it. A classic example of a mentor/teacher, she was engaged by the parents of Helen Keller to teach their blind and deaf seven-year-old child. On March 3, 1887, in Tuscumbia, northern Alabama, she began her mission that would astonish the world. On March 20, 1887, Miss Sullivan wrote:

> *My heart is singing for joy this morning. A miracle has happened! The light of understanding has shone upon my little pupil's mind, and behold, all things are changed.*
>
> *The wild little creature of two weeks ago has been transformed into a gentle child. She is sitting by me as I*

write, her face serene and happy, crocheting a long red chain of Scotch wool.

This belief or faith in tomorrow is eventually translated into the life of the mentee. *The mentor's authority carries weight enough to transmit optimism to the mentee.* We must stay committed to encouraging our mentees until they possess the ability to encourage themselves. Positive affirmation is necessary because of the consistent onslaught of negative input our society gives to mentees.

Fran Tarkenton, former Minnesota Vikings quarterback, once called a play that required him to block onrushing tacklers.

NFL quarterbacks almost never block. They're usually vastly outweighed by defenders, so blocking exposes them to the risk of severe injury.

But the team was behind, and a surprise play was needed. Tarkenton went in to block, and the runner scored a touchdown. The Vikings won the game.

Watching the game films with the team the next day, Tarkenton expected a big pat on the back for what he'd done.

It never came.

After the meeting, Tarkenton approached coach Bud Grant and asked, "You saw my block, didn't you, Coach?" How come you didn't say anything about it?"

Grant replied, "Sure, I saw the block. It was great. But you're always working hard out there, Fran. I figured I didn't have to tell you."

"Well," Tarkenton replied, "if you ever want me to block again, you do!"

May I suggest you review this chapter often? It is central to the task of mentoring, because mentoring is all about speaking into the life of a mentee with authority. Practice the truths listed here and your influence will expand. Blessings on you as you bless others!

How Do I Bring About Change In Someone?

Perhaps you heard the story of the preacher and the taxi cab driver who both died and entered heaven the same day. St. Peter met them at the pearly gate and led them to their mansions. The taxi cab driver was directed to a huge, luxurious mansion; the preacher was then shown his tiny, beaten-up one-room shack. Needless to say, the cabby was elated and the preacher was livid with anger. "I want an explanation!" screamed the clergyman. "You gave the cab driver a mansion, and although I pastored for over forty years in the ministry, you gave me a pitiful shack! How come?" St. Peter smiled. "Well, it's like this," he responded. "Heaven is interested in results. When you preached—people just slept. But, when that man drove—people prayed!"

However fictitious that little story is, the fact of the matter is that heaven is, indeed, interested in results! The key question on that final day will not be: What do you know? Rather it will be: What did you do with what you knew? What truth did we actually apply to our lives? Did we let God change our lives?

One of the key benefits of a good mentor is that they can facilitate growth and, yes, even life change. They help their mentee apply truth to their life.

BUT HOW DO WE DO IT?

Since the goal of our mentoring should be life change, it is imperative for us to understand how change is best fostered in our mentee. When we turn to the pages of scripture, we find the ideal model to follow in the mentoring done by Jesus, the master teacher.

Jesus welcomed people to come to Him for mentoring. He was and is the ultimate mentor. In Matthew 11:28-30, He beckons people who are weary to come to Him for refuge. He then says, "Take my yoke upon you and learn from me, for I am gentle and lowly of heart..." In those days a yoke was used for oxen as they labored in the field. The yoke He spoke of was designed to harness two oxen, a strong one and a weak one. The weaker of the two was present to learn what it meant to work in the field through on-the-job training from the stronger ox. Most of the weight was carried by the strong one until the development process was complete. Wow! What a vivid picture of the mentoring process. Mentees must simply step in and stay in the mentoring process until they are able to do it for someone else.

Obviously, Jesus employed the Hebrew model of learning, as opposed to the Greek model. As I mentioned in Chapter 1, the Greeks had been discipling people for generations prior to Jesus' earthly ministry. Socrates discipled Plato; Plato discipled Aristotle; Aristotle discipled Alexander the Great, and so on. But disciplemaking to the Greeks was a relatively passive exercise in which the mentor instructed his students verbally. They simply sat and received the information. It was academic. It was cognitive and cerebral. It was basically a transmittal of information (philosophy). The Hebrew model was much more experiential. Mark 3:14 states that Jesus chose the twelve disciples "that they might be with Him." It was more than information, it was transformation. They would experience life together as a model and an observer, followed by the observer (disciple) trying it out for himself. It was like the two oxen in a yoke.

Communicating truth happens much more quickly through the Greek model of learning. However, it isn't nearly as effective at changing a life. Students learn more effectively through observation and application than they do sitting in a classroom. Both are necessary.

JESUS' IDEA

I believe we can summarize how Jesus brought about life change by taking the word "IDEA" and allowing it to serve as a reminder of the Hebrew model He employed. The following is how He did it:

I - INSTRUCTION...in a life-related context
(He taught and instructed them verbally.)

D - DEMONSTRATION...in a life related context
(He modeled truths for the disciples to observe.)

E - EXPERIENCE...in a life related context
(He let the disciples participate/apply truth themselves.)

A - ACCOUNTABILITY...in a life related context
(He debriefed their shared experience and assessed their growth.)

Utilizing Jesus' strategy will require you to do more than just talk at your mentee. No doubt your words will be helpful. But, life change will happen more permanently when you:

- ♦ Help them through KNOWING;
- ♦ Help them by SHOWING;
- ♦ Help them to get GOING;
- ♦ Help them see their GROWING.

Why not discuss the topic of evangelism, for instance? Share your struggles with them, as well as your victories. Tell them what you've picked up over the years. Then, why not take them with you on a call to watch you do it? Later, why not push them out of the nest to try it themselves while you observe? Tell them you'll jump in and help them if they need it, but they are to initiate the ministry. Finally, why not sit down and evaluate what was learned through the experience? Assess the growth; correct the mistakes; debrief the truth and hold them accountable to continue in it.

In a nutshell, the whole process can be crystallized by the following age-old process listed below:

- ♦ WE DISCUSS IT.
- ♦ I DO IT, YOU WATCH.
- ♦ WE DO IT TOGETHER.
- ♦ YOU DO IT, I WATCH.
- ♦ WE DEBRIEF.
- ♦ YOU REPEAT THE PROCESS WITH SOMEONE ELSE.

If we mentors will practice this beautiful model, as best we can, we'll find our mentees undergoing transformation. At least that has been my experience. I've seen the pitiful results when

I've failed to do this; I've seen the powerful and positive results when I've successfully done it.

PEOPLE EMPOWERED FOR THE TASK

As you know, when Jesus trained apprentices, He did more than just hand them a job. He empowered them as leaders. We, too, must learn to empower others in our colleges, churches and spheres of influence.

This involves the belief that knowing the mechanics of life and ministry is not enough. We must be fueled from on high with an enabling power, purpose and presence.

WHAT DOES "EMPOWERING" MEAN?

To empower simply means to give your power to someone else. Empowered mentees usually emerge only when someone else has intentionally walked alongside them, investing in and developing them through *demonstration* and *application*. One who empowers has made a commitment to a person, a process, and a purpose that results in the building of an anointed change-agent in the lives of others.

AS A MENTOR YOU EMPOWER WHEN YOU...

1. **Know yourself.**
2. **Know your mentee (areas of strength).**
3. **Clearly define the assignments.**
4. **Teach the "whys" of spiritual growth with the mentee.**
5. **Discuss "process items" with them.**
6. **Spend relational time with them.**
7. **Allow them to watch you minister.**

8. Give them the resources they need.
9. Encourage them to journal through their experience.
10. Hold them accountable for their actions. (Get permission).
11. Give them the freedom to fail.
12. Debrief and affirm regularly.

THE REQUIREMENTS OF EMPOWERING

There are some fundamental requirements for the mentor to empower a mentee. The following ingredients are the nonnegotiables.

1. RELATIONSHIP AND TIME
2. BELIEF IN THE PERSON
3. LOVE EXPRESSED THROUGH LISTENING
4. DISCERNMENT OF NEEDS
5. DEMONSTRATION OF MINISTRY
6. PRAYER FOR GRACE/HOLY SPIRIT
7. AWARENESS OF THE PROCESS

THE RESULTS OF EMPOWERING

1. CONFIDENCE (security)
2. COMPETENCE (ability)
3. CHARACTER (integrity)
4. CHANGE AGENT (influence)

Another great word for empowering is the term "developing." I believe the highest aim we can pursue with mentees is not simply to shepherd them, nor even to equip them for ministry. It must be to develop them to be and do what God has called them to be and do. Shepherding deals with immediate care for their needs, reacting to their cry for help. Equipping deals with proactively preparing them for a task; but developing deals with growing a person to not only mature and serve, but to multiply as well. Note the chart below.

"EMPOWERING PEOPLE"

SHEPHERDING	EQUIPPING	DEVELOPING
Care	Training for ministry	Training for personal growth
Immediate need focus	Task focus	Person focus
Relational	Transactional	Transformational
Service	Management	Leadership
Ministry	Ministry by addition	Ministry by multiplication
Immediate	Short term	Long term
Feeling better	Unleashing	Empowering
Availability	Teaching	Mentoring
Focus on nurture	Focus on specific ministry	Focus on specific leader
No curriculum	Curriculum set	Curriculum flexible
Need oriented	Skill oriented	Character oriented
Maintenance	Doing	Being
What is the problem?	What do I need?	What do they need?
Problem focused	Purpose focused	Person focused
They begin to walk	They'll walk the first mile	They'll walk the second mile

When we commit ourselves to develop our mentees, we will not only change a life, we will have a friend for life. No other investment of our time even touches it. Developing people is strategic; it is biblical; it is multiplicative; and it is the greatest testimony of love for a mentee.

Let me close this chapter with some words from a pastor.

In his book *Who Switched the Price Tags?*, Anthony Campolo related the words of a black Baptist pastor speaking to a group of college students in his congregation. Campolo wrote,

"Children," he said, "you're going to *die!*...One of these days, they're going to take you out to the cemetery, drop you in a hole, throw some dirt on your face, and go back to the church and eat potato salad."

"When you were born," he continued, "You alone were crying and everybody else was happy. The important question I want to ask is this: When you die are you alone going to be happy, leaving everybody else crying? The answer depends on whether you live to gain titles or testimonies. When they lay you in the grave, are people going to stand reciting the fancy titles you earned, or are they going to stand around giving testimonies of the good things you did for them?...Will you leave behind just a newspaper column telling people how important you were, or will you leave crying people who give testimonies of how they've lost the best friend they ever had?"

"There's nothing wrong with titles. Titles are good things to have. But if it ever comes down to a choice between a title or a testimony—go for the testimony."

WHAT ARE THE MOST COMMON PROBLEMS IN MENTORING?

Over the last eighteen years of ministry, I have endured more than my share of problems, challenges and failures in mentoring. Regardless of how much experience I tucked under my belt, new people seemed to always bring new struggles each time a mentor relationship was formed.

Two of my personal failures stand out to me. Perhaps reading about what I learned from them will encourage you. The first took place in 1985. I was supervising the internship program at a large church in southern California. During that year a very real schism occurred between two of my interns; it was a division that, on the surface, appeared to center around their theological differences. I hesitated to step in between them, wanting to allow them to resolve it as adults. By the time I did intervene and determine a resolution, it was too late to salvage one of those relationships. Sean, one of these two young men, was deeply hurt. Out of his pain, he had rallied twenty-five to thirty others who became sympathetic to his perspective. Angry and bitter at my decisions over the issue, Sean left the church, taking the group of twenty-five with him.

Looking back, I now can see that differences in theology

weren't the issue. Sean had no father. His dad had left their family years earlier. My hesitation and subsequent decision had been perceived as one more rejection of him. It appeared that I had taken sides with the other intern. I sat down with him and sought his forgiveness for my leadership failure. I now wish I had taken initiative sooner (i.e., been more proactive); I wish I had exercised deeper discernment (i.e., been more perceptive); and I wish I had defined the values and goals of our ministry more clearly (i.e., communicated priorities). It hurts me to think how unnecessary this struggle really was.

My second big mentoring failure happened right in my home. Arriving home late one evening, I entered through our garage door expecting to find my wife, Pam, at the door to greet me. She wasn't there. I searched the house, only to find she had already gone to bed. When I leaned over to see whether she had fallen asleep yet, I received quite a shock. She was wide awake with tears streaming down her cheeks. Tissues were scattered around her pillow—she had been there a while.

Immediately, I shifted into high gear to fix whatever problem was troubling her. I raced through my mental files hoping to figure out what could be wrong. I was clueless. Finally, I asked, "What's wrong, honey? What happened today?"

She lay still for a moment. Then, she responded quietly, "That's just it, Tim. Nothing happened." I was still in the dark. I asked her to continue. I am sure what she said next hurt her more than it hurt me—and it was horribly painful for me.

"Tim—you're doing such a great job caring for the people at the church," she whispered. "Everyone loves you. And, I don't want to stand in the way of that..." She paused. "But, there is no ministry taking place in our home right now. Nothing is happening in our family—and I feel so alone and forgotten."

Those words shook me up. We both cried for the next forty five minutes. And on that evening, I realized I had failed as a mentor—in the life of the person I cared for most. I had neglected priority one. As a pastor, I had blundered in my ministry to my number one parishioner! With fresh resolve, I made and have maintained a commitment since that evening: If I mentor no one else the rest of my life, I will invest myself in mentoring my wife and two children. Again, more lessons in discernment, initiative and priorities.

THE MOST COMMON PROBLEMS

No doubt, you, too, will experience some tough moments as you attempt to mentor someone. Simply because both of you are human means you'll face some hurdles before the race is over. Along the way, you will notice that there are recurring themes in those hurdles you face. (I certainly did!) You will observe that certain problems surface again and again in human relationships. It has been my experience that four problems emerge as the most common ones between mentors and mentees. Let me list them for you here:

1. **Unmet expectations**
2. **Relationship / personality clashes**
3. **Failure to meet objectives**
4. **Inability / unwillingness to multiply**

Although mentoring difficulties may take on a thousand different shapes and sizes, these four primary categories summarize the majority of them. In this chapter I would like to address each of these briefly, and provide at least some basic guidelines for you as you seek to resolve them in your own mentoring journey.

UNMET EXPECTATIONS

Probably the most common struggle for Generation X, when it comes to authority and organizations, is unmet expectations. Both the baby boomer and the baby buster have grown up with TV and slick marketing which promises the world to them—by noon, tomorrow.

This has led to severe disillusionment within the young adult population. They are disappointed at how often promises are broken and at the lack of integrity leaders seem to possess. When you combine the unrealistic expectations the media fosters in them along with the moral and character failure of many leaders within the established church, you can see we have a real problem on our hands.

Frequently, however, their expectations are unmet because they are *unspoken*. Young and old alike bring emotional baggage to a mentoring relationship that you, as a mentor, have no idea exists. Recognizing this, it is good to employ the principle of proactivity:

> **It is better to build a fence at the top of the cliff than to build a hospital at the bottom.**

The more problems you can resolve before they ever arise, the better off you will be. Let me recommend the following "fence-building" techniques that will enable you to address your mentee's expectations.

1. Clarify the precise purpose at the beginning of your relationship.

Don't leave anything to chance. Give time for both of you to express your "big-picture" goals and desires for the mentoring relationship—up front. Before you ever open up a workbook to study or determine a book of the Bible to read through, talk over your purpose for meeting. I usually invest the first two meetings together to nothing but getting acquainted in this way. Remember, results in mentoring are birthed from relationships.

2. Ask them the top three results they want to gain, from being mentored.

This step breaks down the bigger picture of step one. Ask them to bring a list of items they consider key result areas with them to your next meeting. I generally write these three items down and repeat them back once they've finished articulating them. Sometimes I will even make this list into a covenant that both of us sign—agreeing that we will focus on those items in our times together.

3. Explain your limitations of time and ability.

Take the time to elaborate on how much you realistically can do as a mentor. Sometimes, a mentee is wanting a second father and they become resentful when you fail to fulfill that need in their life. Admit to them that you are *human*. Then detail for them where you believe you are strong and weak in your mentoring experience. This will obviously require you to be secure and emotionally stable; but if you can do it, it will pay off big time. Agree to a relationship that you know you can satisfy in their life. Discuss the kinds of needs you both can meet for each other.

4. Inquire about their past experiences with authority.

Their answer to this question may disclose priceless information to you. Have they struggled with authority figures in their past? What is their relationship like with their dad? How about their teachers or professors? How about former pastors? You get the idea. I began mentoring a young adult years ago, only to discover that they had a huge chip on their shoulder when it came to anyone suggesting how they live their life. We endured some painful conflict that we could have avoided had I known their track record.

5. Pray together regularly about your mutual goals and expectations.

As you continue meeting together, spend time talking to each other and God about how you are doing. Decide you will have a consistent feedback time, and communicate if the relationship is bearing the fruit you had hoped it would. In addition, include God in all of this. Pray aloud together about your desire to meet each other's needs, and remind each other of your love. Make sure they are convinced you have their best interests in mind.

As a mentor, you will want to model right attitudes and appropriate expression of emotion—especially concerning your own unmet expectations. Very likely, there will be times when your mentee will let *you* down. Keep this list in mind as you seek to help your mentee in the relationship process.

RELATIONSHIP AND PERSONALITY CLASHES

A second common hurdle we must jump as mentors is often overlooked at the beginning. I am speaking of personality conflicts with our mentees. Someone once said about marriage: "We fall in love with our spouse's strengths, but we marry their weaknesses." The same is often true about a mentoring relationship. There are certain qualities that draw us to a partner, but it isn't until later that we discover just how human they really are! Just as in marriage, we do not discover these relationship struggles until we're in the midst of the commitment.

A Biblical Example

The fact of the matter is, we ALL have warts and wrinkles. In addition, friction always happens due to these *imperfections*, unwanted *change* and personal *differences*. The Apostle Paul faced this kind of conflict with a man named Philemon. It wasn't so much a personality problem as that they didn't see eye to eye concerning Onesimus, a runaway slave belonging to Philemon. Paul, no doubt, pondered the five options we all face when we get into a sticky relationship conflict. We can respond in one of five ways:

1. I'LL GET THEM!
   (We choose to retaliate and get even; revenge).
2. I'LL GET OUT!
   (We choose escape; we break off and avoid them).
3. I'LL GIVE IN!
   (We choose to surrender and let them have their way).
4. I'LL GO HALF!
   (We choose to compromise and meet halfway).
5. I'LL DEAL WITH IT!
   (We choose to address the issue in a healthy way).

WE MUST REMEMBER...

- Conflict is Natural. (It is going to happen because of our humanity and differences).

- Conflict is Neutral. (It is neither destructive nor constructive in itself).

- Conflict is Normal. (It happens to all of us, strong or weak; you are not alone).

The following steps are the Apostle Paul's course on conflict management. He communicates masterfully with Philemon in his letter and gives us a pattern to follow today. I have broken up the segments of his letter into one word steps below:

1. Compliment (v. 4-7)

Begin by focusing on their positive qualities. Affirm those characteristics that first drew you to your mentor or mentee. Dr. John Maxwell calls this the 101% Principle: find the 1% you agree on or like about them—and give 100% of your attention to it!

2. Compromise (v. 8-13)

Admit early that you are willing to assume some responsibility for the conflict. Recognize the differences in motivation and style, depending upon your temperament (i.e., sanguine, melancholy, phlegmatic or choleric personalities). Determine that you will give in to a degree and meet them halfway. Compromise is not always bad.

3. Choice (v. 14)

Next, lay out the choice that stands in front of you both. You can either flee it, fight it or face it. Determine, if at all possible, to address it and take any steps you can to make the relationship work. Remember the axiom: Friends may come and go in life, but enemies accumulate. Relationships will dissolve unless you work to maintain them.

4. Challenge (v. 15-20)

Extend a clear challenge that they can respond to and maintain their dignity, if possible. Remember, it is more important to win the soul than to win the argument. Lay out good parameters and boundaries you feel are appropriate to make the relationship work.

5. Confidence (v. 21-22)

Finally, end by expressing your sincere confidence in them. Let them know you trust them to make the right decisions and that no personality conflict will prevent you from loving them and caring about their future.

Ann Kiemel Anderson used to repeat a little poem years ago as she described the countless times she found herself in a conflict with someone, or simply wanted to reach out to a person with their "walls" up. It goes like this...

HE DREW A CIRCLE
He drew a circle that shut me out,
Heretic, rebel; a thing to flout;
But love and I had a will to win,
We drew a circle that took him in.

One last word on this subject. In order to preclude personality clashes, I recommend that you use a "Mentor Profile." This is simply a form which potential mentors and mentees can fill out, indicating their hobbies, interests, personality type, goals, motivational needs, leadership style, spiritual gifts, etc. Then, as mentors are matched up with people, you can place people together that seem to fit relationally.

I have provided a sample of my "Mentor Profile" in Chapter 16, which is entitled: How Can I Help My Church Begin Mentoring? Feel free to copy and modify this form to suit your own church ministry.

FAILURE TO MEET OBJECTIVES

This is the third common problem in mentoring. For me, this is the toughest of all mentoring problems. It revolves around the mentee's failure to accomplish a task or assignment, keep a promise, maintain a proper attitude, finish a lesson, or ultimately—to become what you both agreed they would become—a reproducer of the mentoring you have given them.

Let me begin to respond to this problem, by communicating some further "fence-building" steps you can take to prevent this dilemma before it even happens:

1. Have both the mentor and mentee sign a formal covenant together.

This may sound "cheesy" but it has saved many from crashing and burning in their commitment to mentoring. Both partners are to sign a sheet that expresses their commitment to finish the process, including all of the agreed upon assignments. (I have provided a sample Covenant in Chapter 16. Feel free to use it or modify it to fit your personal tastes).

2. Write down the specific, detailed assignments you expect to complete.

Before you begin, make a list of the tasks or assignments in which you might want them to participate. You may not be able to predict all of them, but you will certainly help the mentee get "psyched up" for what lies ahead.

3. Consistently remind them that life is the summation of our choices.

We are all guilty of saying, "I just didn't have the time to do that!" The reality is that we didn't *make the time*. We all have time to do what we believe we must do or want to do. Stephen Covey said it best: The issue is not prioritizing your schedule, but scheduling your priorities. We choose what is important and valuable to us, and the best indicators of those choices are our calendar and our checkbook.

In addition to these, keep the following statements in mind as you consider the discussion with your mentee. They represent the bottom line or the objectives you'll want to embrace in your meeting. These statements are why confronting a failed objective is important.

♦ You want to see them transformed by the power of God.

♦ The goal of confronting them is not condemnation, but restoration.

♦ Challenging them to grow must go beyond giving good advice.

♦ People need help with the practical application of biblical truth.

♦ We must love truth more than anything else in the world.

You may remember Chapter 10 of this book, entitled, "How Do I Confront Effectively?" In that chapter I walk through the steps I take when I need to confront a failed objective, a sin or bad attitude. I want to encourage you to review those eight steps I give in that chapter as a guideline for your own confrontation.

Do your best to embrace these additional principles when meeting with your mentee to confront their failure:

1. BE A GRACE GIVER. All of us need to be believed in, and we never need it more than when we have failed to keep a commitment. Affirm them most as a person when you feel they deserve it least.

2. DISCUSS THE "WHY" BEHIND THE FAILURE.

It may help for you to guide them in their discovery of why they couldn't fulfill an expectation. Was it inability or unwillingness on their part?

3. SEPARATE THE PERFORMANCE FROM THE PERFORMER. Don't connect their failure with their person (i.e., they failed because they are a failure!) Always criticize the performance, not the performer. Failure is an event, not an identity.

4. DEVELOP A PLAN TOGETHER TO PREVENT REPEAT FAILURES. Sit down with a pad of paper and create a game plan for the future. If they have a pattern of failing at a certain task, help them to develop a new pattern.

5. STAY TRUE TO YOUR CONVICTIONS. In your empathy for them, don't compromise what you know is right. The assignment was a good one. Applaud conduct based on character (i.e., doing what is right), not based on feeling (i.e., I felt like doing it).

6. HOLD THEM ACCOUNTABLE. You may be the only one in their life who will take a stand and not let them off the hook of their commitments. Once you've spelled out the goal, talk to them about it consistently. Hold them to finishing what they start.

INABILITY OR UNWILLINGNESS TO MULTIPLY

The ultimate problem or difficulty we face as mentors comes when our mentee fails to apply the truths they learn. In other words, failing to reproduce what they've experienced with you is an abortion of the ultimate goal! We don't mentor others just so they can feel better about themselves—but so that they can turn around and multiply; they are to pass on what they have received (Matthew 10:8). When they refuse to do this, it is a serious spiritual crime in my book!

Consider this: if we do not enable our mentees to go full circle so that they can repeat what we have done with them—we have at least partially failed. Remember, Christian faith is always just one generation away from extinction. Each generation must mentor the willing people of their own time period. Success without a successor is a failure. A true disciple will become a disciple maker.

What You Must Do

There is no foolproof answer to this dilemma. If there were, someone would have packaged it, sold it and made a mint years ago. However, there are some initial steps you can take to preclude this problem. Once again, I direct you to some fence-building action items for the future:

1. Talk about spiritual reproduction from the beginning.

Don't allow your mentee to even begin the process with you without knowing that the expectation is to multiply. They should understand that this is the price tag of receiving so much of your time. Tell them outright that you are assuming they will pass on to their own mentee what they receive from you.

2. Find creative ways to discuss it throughout your mentoring experience.

Don't limit your discussion of this subject to the beginning of your mentoring relationship. Like any vision or conviction, your vision for spiritual reproduction should be communicated consistently and repeatedly. I believe we must:

♦ SEE IT CLEARLY
♦ SHOW IT CONSTANTLY
♦ SAY IT CREATIVELY

3. Locate the stumbling blocks that would prevent multiplication from happening.

Each of us has different reasons for our inability or unwillingness to mentor others. Since we know Jesus has called us to "make disciples of all nations," we know He has called us to be involved in the lives of others. Christianity is all about relationships. Hence, in this step you must probe the heart and head of your mentee, in cooperation with them, and discover why they find it difficult to obey:

• What are their fears?
• What are their weaknesses?
• What is their track record/past experience?

Once you have put your finger on why they seem paralyzed you can pray for them effectively. Then, you can proceed with discussion on a game plan that could enable them to overcome the stumbling block.

Going Deeper

I believe that if you practice the suggestions and truths I communicate in two other chapters in this book, you will successfully defeat this enemy and overcome this obstacle. I'm going to ask you to review the content of the following two chapters:

1. Chapter 14: *How Do I Release a Mentee to Become a Mentor?*

2. Chapter 16: *How Can I Help My Church Begin*

Mentoring?

In Chapter 16, I explain how you can set up a structure for mentoring relationships to be fostered and empowered. It is my belief that without a helpful system for mentoring, 95% of the people that are mentored in our churches will never go on to reproduce. People need structure. We generally don't admit this. In fact, we usually project just the opposite. We say we don't like structure, at least not too much structure. It's too confining, too limiting. Indeed, I'll be the first to admit it can be. I have seen churches who squelch creativity and individuality because of the "sacred" programming in the church. However, in our effort to escape this extreme, we retreat to the other end of the spectrum. We offer no system for developmental relationships—and fail in our efforts to multiply!

Even if your mentee *promises* to find a mentee and replicate your investment in them, the majority of the time they will fail to keep that promise. Unless they are in the unusual top 5% of our evangelical population, they will find themselves unable to follow through for some reason. Most of the time it is due to human infirmity and lack of accountability.

The system I advocate is one which I saw work effectively at the local church where I worked for eleven years in San Diego. I didn't create the system, although I wish I had. It is a system promoted by small group and discipleship gurus all over the world. I have simply modified to fit a mentoring ministry. It involves selecting a Point Person to oversee the ministry. Then, as mentoring relationships come to a close, the graduating mentees qualify to become part of a Mentor Cluster in the church. They are now ready to mentor someone else and join this cluster, even before they may have found their own mentee. This provides ongoing input, encouragement and accountability to reach the goal of multiplication and continued growth. The system, then, looks like this:

MENTOR CLUSTERS

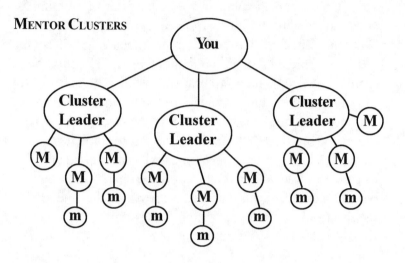

As I mention in Chapter 16, don't be afraid to start small. God does not despise small beginnings. He does not relish *big ministries*, nor does He prefer *small ones*. God simply loves *growing ones*—because growth is a sign of life.

This structure will enable you to grow the mentoring ministry where you are. It will allow you to take it beyond just one generation. It might empower you to leave a legacy.

I trust that the answers to the problems in this chapter will furnish you with a springboard to your own answers. Remember two things. First, the God you serve is always bigger than the problems you face. Second, the reason you endure the hardships we've discussed in this chapter is because mentors are committed to the next generation. If we don't pass on what we possess, others may not get it. We are building the future.

Perhaps this poem says it best. It's called, "The Builder."

THE BUILDER

An old man traveling a lone highway
Came in the evening cold and gray
To a chasm deep and wide.
The old man crossed in the twilight dim,
The sullen stream held no fear for him,
But he stopped when safe on the further side—
And built a bridge to span the tide.

"Old man," said a fellow prilgrim near,
"You are wasting your time in building here,
Your journey will end at the close of the day,
You never again will pass this way,
You've crossed the chasm deep and wide—
Why build this bridge at evening's tide?

The traveler lifted his old gray head,
And to his fellow traveler said:
"There followeth after me today
A youth whose feet must pass this way;
The chasm that's been naught to me,
To that fair youth may a pitfall be;
He, too, must cross in the twilight dim—
Good friend, I am building this bridge for him."

Author Unknown

How Do I Release
A Mentee To
Become A Mentor?

Most of us are familiar with the biography of Helen Keller. Hers is a moving story of a deaf and blind girl who would have grown up a vegetable had it not been for a woman named Anne Sullivan. Because of Anne's work with her, Helen reached adulthood as a changed woman, communicating efficiently, eating by herself and caring for own her personal needs. In the later years of her life, Anne Sullivan had a relapse of a previous condition. She became physically ill and went blind. Now the mentor was in need of someone to work with her. Ironically the one she chose was Helen Keller. Her former disciple had come full circle and was now able to pass on what she had learned.

For nearly two millenniums, the Christian church has known about Jesus' command to make disciples. For almost an equal amount of time, the Church has followed a watered-down methodology for doing it—when we have tried at all. We have diluted this great imperative into a series of passive meetings until we are unclear now as to what a disciple should even look like. We are not reproducing disciple makers through our mentoring; consequently the church-growth movement has registered little or no growth over the last decade. We must begin again to reproduce and multiply.

Releasing a mentee to become a mentor is the crux of our labor as mentors. Before we examine how this is done, let's define what we're aiming for and why. Let's attempt to grasp the biblical vision for spiritual reproduction.

THE TRUTH AND THE MYTH

Let's first dismantle the myths about mentoring and discipleship with a protege. The Church has confused three areas of her life with this art.

Mentoring or disciplemaking is not. . .

MYTH #1: CHRISTIAN EDUCATION
It is not simply the implanting of information for the sake of knowledge. Jesus clarified what made a disciple when He said, "deny yourself, take up your cross, and follow me." (Matthew 16:24) Note that there isn't a word about vast education or knowledge. It was simply servanthood, commitment and purpose.

MYTH #2: COOKIES AND PUNCH
We've often confused fellowship with discipleship, hoping that just getting Christians together will do the trick. If that were true, we would have millions more influential Christians. Fellowship takes place *in the church*; discipleship takes place *in the world*. Mentees who are in the school of life don't need to know what Christianity looks like in the church building, but rather, out in the real world. And. . .it must be intentional.

MYTH #3: SCRIPTURE MEMORIZATION
While some of our mentoring or discipling may include memorizing scripture, it cannot be the crux of it. Intellectual exercises and disciplines aren't enough if our lives don't change. According to John 7:17, Jesus taught that we must first be willing to DO

His will, and only then would we KNOW and understand the teaching. Notice which comes first. Jesus never meant for us to know more than we do.

Mentoring and disciplemaking is. . .

TRUTH #1: THE GREAT COMMISSION

Making disciples is a command to imitate what Jesus did with His twelve. It was a commission, not a suggestion. He mentored those men with His life, then told them to repeat the process themselves. (Matthew 28:19)

TRUTH #2: PARENTING

To mentor or disciple will remind you of the parenting process. This does not mean you are to mother the mentee. What I am saying is that you must invest your life in them. Jesus, in fact, lived with His men and made deposits into their lives on a regular basis. The Apostle Paul even described himself as a father and mother to the Thessalonians in I Thessalonians 2:7-9.

TRUTH #3: MULTIPLICATION THROUGH REPRODUCTION

It is understanding that *adding* to the Church will never be enough if we're going to reach the world. World conquest requires multiplication. If nothing else, the birth rate of the world's population teaches us this. We must multiply disciples through life-on-life reproduction. Listen to Paul's words to Timothy:

And the things that you've received from ME, YOU pass on to FAITHFUL MEN who will be able to teach OTHERS also. (II Timothy 2:2)

Note there are four generations listed above: Paul, Timothy, Faithful Men and Others. That's what mentoring is all about.

EACH ONE MENTOR ONE

Dr. Frank Laubach's epitaph reads:
"The man who taught the world to read"

Dr. Laubach popularized the phrase "Each one teach one." By his simple four-word strategy of teaching one illiterate to read under the condition that they would teach another to read, several million people have now experienced the thrill of reading for the first time. The chain continues to this day, long after his death.

TRY TO IMAGINE...

Pause for 60 seconds right now and try to imagine the implications of the mentoring relationship. What if each leader, over a lifetime, mentored 12 people, as Jesus did?
You mentor 12. . .who mentor 12 equals 144!
who mentor 12 equals 1,728!
who mentor 12 equals 20,736!
who mentor 12 equals 248,832!
who mentor 12 equals 2,985,984!

IS AN UNBROKEN CHAIN OF MENTORS REALISTIC?

Probably not! But the point is clear. Even if only a small fraction of mentors and mentees follow through, an extremely significant difference in the number of leaders in the twenty-first century would be made.

Today, the future governor of your state or the future president of our nation may be in your scout troop, Sunday school class, college, or youth group at church.

Multiplication brings exponential growth. The gentleman who created the game of checkers understood this. This inventor was summoned to visit the King (since he resided within the monarchy), and he was thanked for the game. In fact, the King offered him up to a third of his Kingdom. The inventor thought for a moment and then made his request. He asked for one grain of corn for the first square on his checkerboard; two for the second; four for the third; then eight; then sixteen, then thirty-two; etc. It was exponential increases. But the King didn't see it. He was livid with anger over such a small request. Little did he know the grains that would be required to fill the last square was such an enormous number—his Kingdom didn't even have that much corn!

WHAT WAS SUPPOSED TO HAPPEN WITH US

Jesus set the pattern, deliberately, through His work with the twelve. He modeled the Hebrew style of teaching and learning by life-investment, on-the-job training. After three-and-a-half years, He launched the disciples to do it on their own. He re-issued an Old Testament commission to take this relationship with God to the whole earth. To reach the earth, they were to identify a cluster of people—and one life at a time—multiply throughout every nation. He had given them every resource they needed, including His example with them, and the presence of the Holy Spirit to remind and empower them to imitate it.

It was an aggressive and offensive strategy that He fully expected them to carry out (Matthew 16:18-19). Interestingly, up until the second century—they did. After four to six generations, however, the pattern began to fade. And in 313 A.D., the Great Commission was dealt a tragic blow, ironically, by a confessed Christian man. Constantine, emperor of the Roman empire, issued a declaration that all citizens and government workers were to become Christians; his empire was to automatically become a Christian one. Immediately, the authenticity and the cost of truly imitating Jesus was watered down. The standard was lowered, and the meaning of "Christian" began its spiral downward.

Obviously, this is no excuse for true Christians to cease being and making disciples. However, coupled with this event, the church began to face the emergence of four other factors that hindered the making of disciples, and caused them to drop the ball.

WHY WE DROPPED THE BALL

1. HUMAN NATURE
    (We migrate toward comfort zones and the path of least resistance.)

2. CLERGY VS. LAITY DISTINCTION
    (The clergy thought *they* were the church; the laity became the "idiots!" The latin root word for "laity" is the word " idiot.")

3. INSTITUTIONALISM
    (The church became a cold, sterile, impersonal corporation. Professionals were paid to do ministry.)

4. THE GREEK LEARNING MODEL
    (The church embraced an academic, passive, educational model instead of the Hebrew model of developmental relationships.)

Clearly, we must return to the blueprint, the pattern that Jesus set for us.

HOW DO WE DO IT?

In this chapter, I have used the terms disciplemaking and mentoring interchangeably. There are some differences, no doubt. But when we mentor in order to reproduce other mentors, the steps begin to look very similar to discipleship. Consider this definition:

Disciplemaking involves a developmental relationship, where a strong, reproductive Christian invests in a willing apprentice, so that he/she not only obtains the character/lifestyle but also becomes a multiplying Christian.

GETTING STARTED

As you commit yourself to obeying Jesus' strategy, consider the following sequence of steps:

1. **Pray for conviction and vision.**
2. **Select a person or group from your following to be a mentee.**
3. **Cast vision to them for spiritual reproduction (they will mentor someday).**
4. **Ask for commitment.**
5. **Be prepared and set goals. (Create lesson plans)**
6. **Meet regularly for a set time.**
7. **Obey and apply the lessons together.**
8. **Invest yourself in the person and process.**
9. **Help them find a potential mentee.**
10. **Evaluate and launch them to try it themselves.**

TWELVE FACTORS IN MENTORING/ DISCIPLEMAKING

When Jesus determined to choose twelve men to mentor, He prayed all night. Following that prayer time, He hand-picked his proteges/disciples. As we see Him mentoring through His three-and-a-half year ministry, we see a model mentor. He not only brings about positive life change in them, but prepares them to become mentors/disciplers, as well. I spotted the following factors that Jesus implemented with his twelve. Read these over and study the scripture passages that illustrate the twelve factors.

1. INITIATIVE (Luke 6:12-13)
2. PROXIMITY (Mark 3:14/Luke 8:1)
3. FRIENDSHIP (John 15:15)
4. EXAMPLE (John 13:15)
5. COMMITMENT (Matthew 16:24/John 13:1)
6. RESPONSIBILITY (Mark 6:7)
7. KNOWLEDGE (Luke 8:9-10)
8. VISION (Matthew 4:19/John 4:35)
9. TRUST (Matthew 10:1-8)
10. EVALUATION (Luke 10:17-24)
11. POWER (John 20:22/Acts 1:8)
12. LAUNCH (Matthew 28:18-20)

YOU JUST MIGHT CHANGE THE WORLD

It's true. Making a commitment to take your mentee full circle and reproduce spiritually could change the world. It certainly did with Jesus and the twelve. It has also happened various times through history. John Wesley founded the Methodist church on this principle. Even in the twentieth century, movements have begun when men have mentored in this manner.

Dawson Trotman is a beautiful example. "Daws" was the founder of The Navigators, a worldwide ministry committed to making disciples. Early in his ministry, a young sailor approached Daws and asked for help with personal growth. Daws clarified that what the sailor was really asking for was to be discipled. He then agreed to do it over the next several months. During the experience, this sailor's life was so dramatically changed that he brought a buddy of his to Daws and asked if Daws would disciple him as well. The reply startled both of the sailors: "Absolutely not." Then, Daws went on to say, "If your friend is going to be discipled, it will have to be you who does it." So the two of them connected in a discipleship relationship. Upon their completion, the chain continued. Both went out and found someone in whom they could invest their lives. This happened again and again and again.

What makes this story so intriguing is that it literally transformed the atmosphere on the ship. Eventually, the F.B.I. was called to investigate what was going on. Some thought a cult had broken out. Others wondered about the odd behavior of what was once a normal group of sailors. Clearly, things were different. What's more, once the F.B.I. began to investigate, it took them six months to sift through all the men who had been discipled in order to find Daws—the one who had started the whole thing.

That is one thick web of disciples! What an encouraging snapshot of what could happen if we became serious about multiplying. We must remember, however, that spiritual reproduction happens one life at a time. God doesn't despise small beginnings. Be committed to starting a movement as opposed to a program. Programs usually start big, then fizzle and become small. Movements usually start small (remember Jesus' twelve disciples?) and become huge. Jesus took that tiny group of mentees and, after pouring His life into them, pushed them out of the nest to fly. The world has never been the same since.

I think He had the right idea.

How Do We Gain From Historical Mentors?

The good news about mentoring is that it can be done somewhat effectively at a distance. Mentors don't have to live nearby, nor do they even have to be alive to speak into our lives today.

Through the consumption of books, particularly biographies, we can be mentored by Christianity's greatest leaders from the past. Ted Engstrom comments on this by writing:

Some books, wrote Francis Bacon a century ago, are to be tasted, others to be swallowed, and some few to be chewed and digested. Worthy books are like mentors—available as companions and as solitude for refreshment. Thomas Carlyle, in his essays, noted that if time is precious, no book that will not improve by repeated readings deserves to be read at all. I have set a goal to read a book each week, and I can't imagine my life without the companionship of these faithful mentors.

A book is good if it is opened with expectation and closed with profit. The books you choose say much about you. Don't be a one-issue reader. Read widely—even books by authors with whom you disagree. Taste some, chew some, and digest the best. And your children will do the same.

Abraham Lincoln's life illustrates beautifully the value of books as mentors. These storehouses of knowledge carried him through disappointments that would have shattered a weaker man. Among the troubles that visited him were the death of his mother when he was only nine, rejection by his first love, the bankruptcy of his first business venture, defeat the first time he sought public office. Even when he finally made it to Congress, he lasted only one term, being so unpopular that reelection was out of the question. At that point in his life he told a friend, "I will get ready. My time will come."

Remember Abraham Lincoln when you look at your protege and are tempted to give up. Next to praying "Thy will be done," I can't think of a better expression of faith than, "I will get ready. My time will come."

HOW TO BENEFIT FROM BIOGRAPHIES

My good friend and co-laborer Steve Moore shares the following insights regarding mentors from the past.

Historical role models provide us with a source of passive mentoring from which all Christians may benefit. Regardless of our circumstances, we can surround ourselves with brilliant thinkers, visionaries and hot-hearted disciples of Jesus by reading biographical accounts of great leaders from church history.

It is how we approach the reading of these works and what we learn from them that is important. Exciting true events unfold within the covers of biographies. However, entertainment should not be our motivation for reading them. Neither should we look at these leaders as antiquated players in history, relevant only to their time and location. We need to evaluate their lives from various perspectives with the intention of learning practical lessons that will empower us to become world changers today. Here are some pointers gleaned over the years on how to benefit from biographies.

1. *Maintain a perspective as to where the mentor fits in history.* Disassociating historical mentors from their place in history robs us of an important sense of perspective. Questions about the socio-political climate of a historical mentor's world need to be answered in order for us to meaningfully process the events of their life. It is usually helpful to construct a leadership time line and develop the historical setting out of which the time line arises. A leadership time line might include a series of phases such as foundations, inner-life growth, ministry, and maturity. The length of each phase will vary and might span a decade or more. Such a time line would include important events in the individual's life as well as important historical events. This will allow you to evaluate the impact history had on the individual as well as the individual's impact on history.

   For example, Samuel Mills' mother offered him to God for missionary service as a young boy. This is a noble act of faith in any generation. But when she did it, there were no North American mission agencies, and no one from this continent had gone out as a missionary! No wonder the idea stuck in young Samuel's mind. He eventually did play an important role in the formation of the first North American mission board along with the sending of America's first missionaries!

2. *Read with a sense of purpose—know what you are looking for.* Identify the process items of each stage in

the historical mentor's time line. Process items include the ways and means used by God to move a person toward leadership. They may be events, people, circumstances, interventions, or inner-life lessons. (If you would like to know more about the term "process item," read Robert Clinton's book, *The Making of a Leader*.) Look for clues to their leadership style, how they implement change, deal with failure or opposition. Make note of their methods. Were they innovators, reformers, or pioneers? Did they make extraordinary sacrifices or face difficult suffering?

3. *Become a member of the historical mentor's inner circle.* Most great leaders get close to only a handful of people. The higher up the leadership ladder they climb, the more inaccessible they become to the broad base of their constituency. But through a biography you can literally move into the inner circle of leaders who surrounded a historical mentor. You can sit in on board meetings, listen to private conversations, read personal letters and journal entries!

Just imagine you were given the opportunity to spend a week with James Dobson, Chuck Colson, Bill Bright, Loren Cunningham, or the leader of your choice. You could not ask questions—only follow the leader and observe—at home, in the office, on the road, wherever they go. Would you do it? Of course you would! Future generations will probably get this opportunity by way of biographical writings. But you can access the inner circle of hundreds of great leaders—not just for a week, but for the better part of a lifetime.

4. *Identify the important windows of opportunity in the*

historical mentor's life. In the developmental stages of most leaders, there are a few key windows of opportunity through which the primary focus of their ministry is opened. Much can be learned from identifying and evaluating those key moments. How did God prepare the mentor for these opportunities? How long did they prepare? Did they have a sense of destiny regarding their ministry focus? How rapidly did their ministry unfold after the windows of opportunity were opened? What were the key factors in their decision to take new steps of faith?

5. *Identify the historical mentor's ultimate contribution.* The term, "ultimate contribution" comes from the studies of leadership emergence theory at Fuller Seminary School of World Mission. An ultimate contribution is defined as a lasting legacy of a Christian worker for which they are remembered and which furthers the cause of Christianity by one or more of the following: setting standards for life and ministry; impacting lives by enfolding them in God's Kingdom or developing them once in the Kingdom; serving as a stimulus for change; leaving behind an organization, institution or movement that serves as a channel through which God can work; or the discovery or promotion of ideas and communication that further God's work.

When evaluating the lives of historical mentors, there are scores of potential categories for ultimate contributions. A specific research project identified twelve primary categories for ultimate contributions or lasting legacies from the lives of missionaries. These twelve categories are listed in the following chart.

Ultimate Contribution/Lasting Legacy	Thrust of contribution
Saint	living a model life
Stylistic Practitioner	demonstrating a model ministry style
Mentor	productive ministry with individuals
Public Rhetorician	productive ministry with large groups
Crusader	right wrongs and injustices in society
Artist	creative breakthroughs
Founder	starts new organizations
Stabilizer	solidifies organizations
Researcher	develops new ideation
Writer	captures new ideation for the use of others
Promoter	distributes effectively new ideation
Pioneer	founds apostolic type works

Keep in mind that there will likely be some overlap between these categories, and most leaders will make more than one ultimate contribution.

6. *Keep a quote on file that summarizes a main principle you have gleaned from the historical mentor.*

Many people have read biographies of great leaders but can remember very little, if anything, about them. One of the best ways to glean the most from historical mentors is by collecting quotes that summarize a key principle from their lives. If you do not actually memorize a quote, try to at least learn the details of an important vignette from the historical mentor's life.

It is helpful to write down a quote and share it with other people for several months as a means of reinforcing it. While you are learning the details of a vignette, share them with others for as long as it takes to lock them into your memory.

SOME LASTING EXAMPLES

In my devotional book, The Greatest Mentors In The Bible, I attempt to summarize what we can learn today from the mentors found in the scripture. I found thirty-two mentoring relationships in the Old and New Testaments—from Abraham and Lot, to Jethro and Moses, to Paul and Timothy. Clearly, we can learn from each of these relationships and gain some handles for our lives today.

My point is, we can be mentored by any leader—even those in the scriptures—if we'll let them speak into our lives and influence the direction we are heading. In order to do this, we must approach them as mentors, not just stories from the Bible. I challenge you to do just that.

How Can
I Help My Church
Begin Mentoring?

Many of you who read this book or use it as a reference guide, long for your church to begin a formal mentoring ministry. You have prayed that God would get hold of your pastor's heart and raise up a point person to lead the way. You are convinced, deep down, that if people would just commit themselves to this kind of developmental relationship, lives would change and so would the atmosphere of the church.

I have some good news for you. I agree. Furthermore, in this chapter I will lay out some guidelines for you to pursue this lofty vision. I must warn you of something, however. If you apply the material you are about to read, it will force you to think big! It may even cause you to re-examine your own values. Your hunger for mentoring may have begun with a self-serving purpose; you knew that you needed a mentor. I am going to challenge you to think beyond your own needs now and focus on your church family or college or whatever organization you are a part of right now. I want you to ask yourself: What realistic steps could you take to facilitate a mentoring ministry that might impact the next several generations? Once you've answered that question, let me share with you what I think will enable you to participate in a successful beginning.

THE NECESSARY INGREDIENTS

God reminds us in the Old Testament to not "despise small beginnings." As you consider helping your church begin a mentoring ministry, probably the worst thing you could do is insist that it begin with a huge, churchwide "blow-out" rally where everyone is encouraged to jump in and get involved. This is how we envision many successful new programs in the church. May I remind you—you are not starting a *program*—you are on the front end of a *movement*. Remember my words early in this book: programs usually start big and then fizzle when their novelty has waned. Movements usually start small and grow very big because they begin at a grass roots level. Jesus began a *movement* with twelve men, not a program. Please hear what I am saying. It is best to begin small, with a committed core of people.

When bakers begin the process of baking a cake, they usually take a gander at the list of ingredients they will need. They get the big picture of what they are getting themselves into before they turn the oven on. I think we ought to begin the same way. The following are the ingredients I believe you will eventually need if a mentoring ministry is going to succeed in your church.

1.   A Point Person. Someone will have to offer leadership, cast vision and own the responsibility for helping the ministry get off the ground. This person is the key spokesperson for the vision. They must live and breathe mentoring.

2.   A Mentoring Structure or System. While mentoring may begin with just a handful of loosely knit people, it will not continue to grow unless you implement some kind of structure for people to enter. This system will enable things to continue after you're gone.

3. A Vehicle for Enlisting. I suggest you design a "Mentoring Match-up Form" for all persons who want to sign up for mentoring. This form will help prevent relational "train wrecks" and improve the chances of success. I provide one later in this chapter.

4. A Written Commitment that People Agree Upon. Mentoring is a broad subject. There must be unity around the vision. You will invite chaos and disappointment unless you develop a covenant people can read and sign to know what they are getting in to.

5. A Healthy Approach. Finally, you must take the right approach in order to see this movement get off the ground. Your approach to a new idea can make it or break it. At the close of this chapter I will suggest some healthy steps you can take.

Let's take a look at each one of these ingredients, one by one. I will do my best to give you samples or suggestions of how each one can be achieved.

A POINT PERSON

Dr. John Maxwell has said, "Everything rises and falls on leadership." Even if that statement were an exaggeration, you could not argue that *most* of the success of any ministry rests on the ability of the one who leads it.

This illustrates vividly how important it is for the right point person to be selected for this new mentoring ministry. Ideally, they should have an evident anointing on them from God for this calling. They should have favor with the people in the church, particularly the potential constituents of the ministry itself. They should know how to communicate vision (a little charisma wouldn't hurt!). They should have the gift of faith to think beyond a one-generation ministry, and they should be willing to pay the price to set this ministry in motion. First gear always requires more work than fourth gear. Momentum may be our best friend, but getting it often takes hard labor!

The point person would ideally be an influencer within the church or organization. They should be perceived by the people as credible and worthy of following. It is helpful for them to be well liked and respected. When they speak—people listen. J. Oswald Sanders provided us with the greatest one word definition for leadership when he said: Leadership is influence. Period. This is the optimal point person profile. Pray for God to raise up such a person, and don't eliminate yourself from His list of possibilities!

I mentioned one of the fundamental truths of mentoring earlier in this book when I said, *"We teach what we know, but we reproduce what we are."* Because this is true, you must be careful in the selection of this point person. The people who enlist in the ministry, and even the ministry itself, will begin to reflect the personality and values of the leader. The ministry's breadth and depth, its flavor and speed, its attraction and reputation will almost all be dependent on the person who spearheads the operation.

For this reason, may I suggest an acrostic for the point person and every other leader who participates in your mentoring ministry? Mentors are PROVIDERS. They provide for the mentees who watch and follow them. Hence, I believe the word PROVIDER will serve as a terrific ministry profile for this point person. Note the following qualities:

A MENTOR / POINT PERSON MUST BE...

P - PURPOSEFUL

From now on you can no longer be casual about the people and relationships around you. Because there are people following, you must live and serve on purpose, not by accident.

R - RELATIONAL

Sometimes this doesn't come naturally, especially for men. However, because mentoring is about relationships, you must learn to model healthy relationships.

O - OBJECTIVE

As a leader or mentor, you cannot afford to allow your personal tastes to interfere with doing what is right. You must objectively assess people, relationships, mentor matchups.

V - VULNERABLE

Another area you must model is the area of self disclosure, transparency, honesty and relational vulnerability. Our mentees are going to emulate our level of openness.

I - INCARNATIONAL

Incarnation means "to become flesh." A mentor or point person cannot merely talk the talk, but must exemplify the kind of life and ministry they desire from their followers.

D - DEPENDABLE

Regardless of your past inconsistencies, from now on you, as a leader, must be absolutely dependable and responsible to those who work with you and under you.

E - EMPOWERING

You must take on a style that is empowering to those around you. To empower means to give your power away. You must delight in and facilitate the successes of your followers.

R - RESOURCEFUL

Perhaps above all, you must be resourceful with every tool God has given you. For the progress of the Kingdom, use wisely every person, dollar and opportunity you have.

One more thought. This point person does not need to emerge from the very beginning, although that would be helpful. He or she must simply step forward or be chosen by the time the church is ready to communicate the vision to a larger constituency than the committed core group. At this point, someone must assume responsibility for the health and development of the movement.

A MENTORING STRUCTURE OR SYSTEM

The second ingredient that must be included in our recipe is a system that will facilitate a growing ministry. As I mentioned earlier, most of us attached a negative connotation to the word "structure" or "system." They sound confining, like they might quench the work of the Holy Spirit. However, if you read about the great leaders in the Bible, you will find, almost without fail, that they worked a strategy. For instance, there was a method in Jesus' training of His disciples AND for the Apostle Paul implementing his church planting strategy...*and neither quenched the Holy Spirit!* There was structure to their ministry.

Consider this. You will only grow your ministry to the size of one person unless you create some structure that invites other people into it. In fact, I will suggest you need structure for the following reasons:

A. You want the ministry to expand and grow, to reach many people you may not know.

B. You don't want to lose track of who and where each mentor and mentee is serving.

C. You want each person to stay involved and begin mentoring after they are mentored.

D. You want new people to enter the ministry easily and in an organized fashion.

If you agree with the statements above, then keep reading. I would like to introduce a system to you that is relational yet organized. It is one that places mentors in small groups for support and accountability, and it exemplifies the Hebrew learning model in the process. Notice the diagram below that illustrates how this system looks:

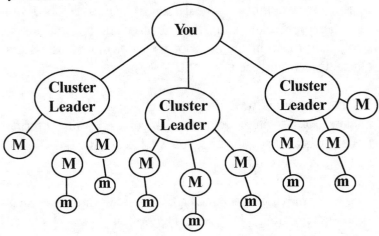

In the diagram, you see words and letters. The large circle with the word "YOU" in the middle is the point person. The circles with the words "Cluster Leader" are the facilitators of mentoring clusters. These cluster leaders are really mentors to the mentors. They meet with the mentors once a month for sup-

port and accountability. These clusters are ideal not only to provide ongoing training and input for current mentors, but also for
mentees who've just finished being mentored and now need some
consistent encouragement to reproduce. The capital letter **"M"**
is for the mentors who are in the cluster. Each of them is attached
to a mentee (one to one or small group), who is signified by the
lower case **"m."** Mentors meet with their mentees as often as
they choose—weekly, bi-weekly, etc.

In short, you may begin with just two or three mentors meeting with their mentees. But as the ministry grows, you select
cluster leaders to coordinate graduating mentees and current
mentors, meeting with them monthly for support and accountability. I suggest you put no more than six to eight mentors per
cluster, since it would be difficult for a cluster leader to shepherd
more than that number. The goal is, once anyone is finished with
their mentoring relationship, they are placed in a mentor cluster.
Obviously, the more mentors you have, the more clusters and
cluster leaders you need.

You can quickly see that the point person, and the cluster
leaders are all strategic selections. If you find good nurturing
leaders to head up the clusters, you will likely have a successful,
ongoing mentoring ministry.

Before moving on, let me share some final words of encouragement regarding this system. I have seen it work in several
locations across the country. It has worked best when the following action steps were included:

1.   Have your clusters meet with their cluster leaders in homes.
It's usually a warmer, more relaxed atmosphere than the church
building.

2. Serve food. Food always helps break down any relational barriers. Light snacks that can be consumed while you are discussing issues are ideal.

3. Meet regularly. A rhythm of meetings that is predictable is optimal, such as the first Monday night of the month, etc. Do your best not to disrupt this rhythm.

4. Be sure the cluster leader is well prepared for each meeting. Remember, they are the mentors for the mentors. Each meeting ought to be excellent and provide incentive for the mentors to show up, whether it's the fellowship, the training, the prayer support, etc. You may want to discuss issues relevant to mentors, like confrontation, motivation, etc.

5. With the direction of the cluster leader, consider good match-ups for the new mentors needing to find mentees. Wise counsel often comes from such a group of experienced people.

A VEHICLE FOR ENLISTING

The third ingredient you'll want to add to the recipe for a successful mentoring ministry is the creation of a vehicle for enlisting people. Once you've moved beyond the first generation or two, you'll be ready to invite others into the mentoring experience. One common challenge you'll face at this point is the matching up of potential mentees and mentors. How do you know they'll like each other? What if they don't sense good chemistry between them? Can you prevent relational "train wrecks" before they occur?

I believe you can help yourself immensely by creating a "Mentor Match-up" form for any person interested in getting involved—whether they'll be a mentor or mentee. This form allows them to put on paper their goals, personality and style, hobbies and interests, spiritual gifts, etc. in order to be placed with a compatible partner.

Whenever someone expresses an interest in being mentored or becoming a mentor, simply give them this form and put the ball in their court. You respond to them only after they have filled out the form. This will be one way to discover just how interested they really are.

Notice the sample form (*Exhibit 16-1*) I have provided for you at the end of this chapter. It can be typed and formatted easily on one 8½" x 11" page, front and back. Look it over carefully. It allows for a person to communicate whether they are looking for a mentor or mentee; their hobbies/interests, their motivational needs, leadership style, temperament, etc. Each of these answers can be obtained by taking the simple tests provided on the next few pages. The results of each of the tests reveal information helpful to your matching them with the appropriate partner. For instance, note the following descriptions:

1. Temperament Test (*Exhibit 16-2*).
This simple test, designed by Florence Littauer, lets you know their personality type. It is based on Hyppocrites, the Greek philosopher, and his studies of the four major personalities: Sanguine, Melancholy, Phlegmatic and Choleric.

2. Motivational Needs Survey (*Exhibit 16-3*).
These results tell you what motivates the person most: completing a task, relating with people or influencing a group. Each of us has different combinations of motivational needs that are good to know at the beginning.

3. Spiritual Gifts Test.

I chose not to provide this test since there are so many already available on the market and because churches differ so widely on which test is appropriate. In any case, it will inform you as to the person's spiritual gifts (abilities).

Be sure and have every person who fills out this Mentor Match-up form be as thorough as possible. The more you know, the better chance you'll have of placing them in the right mentoring relationship. The goals of the mentor and mentee should obviously match, but don't be afraid of putting opposites together, in terms of personalities, as long as they know you are doing this for the sake of their growth and development. Once you match two people together, suggest that they meet twice just to get acquainted and to see if they have compatible expectations and styles.

A WRITTEN COMMITMENT THAT PEOPLE AGREE UPON

A fourth ingredient I've found helpful in mentoring ministry is a written agreement or covenant that both the mentor and the mentee sign.

This covenant allows the two individuals to declare formally their intention to follow through and remain committed to the relationship and the goals laid out in the beginning. The covenant does not need to be elaborate, but should state the basic values of the mentoring ministry and what the goals are.

Every one of us has made a commitment in the past that we have failed to keep. It is frustrating. It can be embarrassing. This signed agreement empowers the parties to publicly become accountable to each other and the others in the ministry. It increases the likelihood of finishing what they started and reduces the drop-out rate. It is not foolproof, but it is the closest thing to foolproof you'll ever find with a group of volunteers.

Notice the sample covenant provided in *Exhibit 16-4*. In addition to the actual covenant, I have also provided a list of possible covenant guidelines in *Exhibit 16-5*. This could be handed out to each person who will sign the covenant as a confirmation of the values and common ground rules everyone has agreed to follow.

A HEALTHY APPROACH

The final ingredient our recipe calls for is a healthy approach. This means you will initiate your approach to this mentoring ministry in the church in a mature way, and in full submission to the God given leaders in that church.

It could be very easy to do end runs around the established leadership, especially if they don't share your passion for mentoring. Don't do it. Be patient. Slow down if you need to, but don't play the role of the renegade or maverick who bulldozes over everyone in the way. You cannot force this ministry into being. You and God and the leadership of the church must work cooperatively. This is the optimal method in His Kingdom.

No doubt, the practice of mentoring can make a big difference in your church. However, it may not do so right away. It should generally start at the grass-roots level, with one or two mentors investing in one life at a time. Remember, God does not despise small beginnings!

My suggestion would be to begin small, but plan some infrastructure for mentoring to continue as new generations of people finish being mentored and go on to mentor someone else. Consider the following list as a sequence of steps:

1. **Pray for you and your church to own the vision for mentoring.**

2. **Define the commitment and plan on paper. (Both short and long term).**

3. **Seek the blessing of the church leadership.**

4. **Select a person or group from your sphere of influence to mentor.**

5. **Invest in your mentee: the person, process and purpose.**

6. **Challenge your mentee to reproduce when they finish.**

7. **Train and release your mentee to challenge their own mentee.**

8. **Choose (or become) the point person for the mentor ministry.**

9. **Develop a form for mentor match-ups.**

10. **Establish a structure for mentor clusters. (See earlier chart.)**

11. **Create a system for interested people to sign up.**

12. **Find places to communicate the vision to the congregation.**

As you can see, this practical list of twelve steps includes each of the ingredients I have listed earlier. I am recommending that you follow this list in the basic order I have given it. If you find it difficult to wade through these steps alone, find a confidant who can provide some emotional and spiritual support as you pioneer this ministry.

Don't forget that the journey of a thousand miles begins with a single step. May God bless you as you step out and begin to influence your church family, through mentoring, for the cause of Christ!

Exhibit 16-1

MENTOR MATCH-UPS
Profile

Name _____ Phone _____

Address/City/Zip _____

Age _____ Sex _____ Birthday _____ Marital Status _____

Are you looking for: A Mentor   A Mentee   (circle one)

PERSONAL PROFILE

Hobbies/Interests _____

Personality Profile _____

Motivational Needs _____

Leadership Style _____

Spiritual Gifts _____

How often do you want to meet with a partner in a mentoring relationship? (circle)

Once A Week   Twice A Week   Once A Month   Twice A Month

Past discipleship/mentoring experience: _____

_____

Goals: List three things you'd like to accomplish with the help of a mentor/mentee:

1. _____

2. _____

3. _____

FOR MENTORS ONLY

List three areas of strength you can pass on to someone, such as modeling prayer, evangelism, decision making, parenting, organization, priority setting, etc.

1. _____

Exhibit 16-1

2. _____

3. _____

In their book, *Connecting*, Paul Stanley and Robert Clinton outline seven different kinds of mentoring roles. To help us properly match you with someone, please circle one or two roles for which you feel best suited.

1. Discipler: Helping with the basics of following Christ.
2. Spiritual Guide: Accountability; direction/insight for maturation.
3. Coach: Motivation; skills needed to meet a task or challenge.
4. Counselor: Timely advice; perspective on self, others, ministry.
5. Teacher: Knowledge and understanding of a specific subject.
6. Sponsor: Career guidance; protection; relational networking.
7. Model: Personal model or example for life, ministry or career.

FOR MENTEES ONLY...

List three areas in which you would most appreciate the help of a mentor, such as time management, spiritual walk, career choices, ministry, etc.

1. _____

2. _____

3. _____

CONCERNS AND COMMENTS

Any final communication that will foster a good mentor match up...

_____

_____

_____

_____

Exhibit 16-2

DIRECTIONS – IN EACH OF THE FOLLOWING ROWS OF FOUR WORDS ACROSS, PLACE AN **X** IN FRONT OF THE ONE WORD THAT MOST OFTEN APPLIES TO YOU. CONTINUE THROUGH ALL FORTY LINES. BE SURE EACH NUMBER IS MARKED.

STRENGTHS

#				
1	Adventurous	Adaptable	Animated	Analytical
2	Persistent	Playful	Persuasive	Peaceful
3	Submissive	Self-sacrificing	Sociable	Strong-willed
4	Considerate	Controlled	Competitive	Convincing
5	Refreshing	Respectful	Reserved	Resourceful
6	Satisfied	Sensitive	Self-reliant	Spirited
7	Planner	Patient	Positive	Promoter
8	Sure	Spontaneous	Scheduled	Shy
9	Orderly	Obliging	Outspoken	Optimistic
10	Friendly	Faithful	Funny	Forceful
11	Daring	Delightful	Diplomatic	Detailed
12	Cheerful	Consistent	Cultured	Confident
13	Idealistic	Independent	Inoffensive	Inspiring
14	Demonstrative	Decisive	Dry humor	Deep
15	Mediator	Musical	Mover	Mixes Easily
16	Thoughtful	Tenacious	Talker	Tolerant
17	Listener	Loyal	Leader	Lively
18	Contented	Chief	Chartmaker	Cute
19	Perfectionist	Permissive	Productive	Popular
20	Bouncy	Bold	Behaved	Balanced

Exhibit 16-2

WEAKNESSES

#				
21	___ Blank	___ Bashful	___ Brassy	___ Bossy
22	___ Undisciplined	___ Unsympathetic	___ Unenthusiastic	___ Unforgiving
23	___ Reticent	___ Resentful	___ Resistant	___ Repetitious
24	___ Fussy	___ Fearful	___ Forgetful	___ Frank
25	___ Impatient	___ Insecure	___ Indecisive	___ Interrupts
26	___ Unpopular	___ Uninvolved	___ Unpredictable	___ Unaffectionate
27	___ Headstrong	___ Haphazard	___ Hard to please	___ Hesitant
28	___ Plain	___ Pessimistic	___ Proud	___ Permissive
29	___ Angered easily	___ Aimless	___ Argumentative	___ Alienated
30	___ Naive	___ Negative attitude	___ Nervy	___ Nonchalant
31	___ Worrier	___ Withdrawn	___ Workaholic	___ Wants credit
32	___ Too sensitive	___ Tactless	___ Timid	___ Talkative
33	___ Doubtful	___ Disorganized	___ Domineering	___ Depressed
34	___ Inconsistent	___ Introvert	___ Intolerant	___ Indifferent
35	___ Messy	___ Moody	___ Mumbles	___ Manipulative
36	___ Slow	___ Stubborn	___ Show-off	___ Skeptical
37	___ Loner	___ Lord over	___ Lazy	___ Loud
38	___ Sluggish	___ Suspicious	___ Short-tempered	___ Scatterbrained
39	___ Revengeful	___ Restless	___ Reluctant	___ Rash
40	___ Compromising	___ Critical	___ Crafty	___ Changeable

NOW TRANSFER ALL YOUR X'S TO THE CORRESPONDING WORDS ON THE PERSONALITY SCORING SHEET AND ADD UP YOUR TOTALS.

Reprinted from PERSONALITY PLUS, Florence Littauer, Fleming H. Revell Publishers.

Exhibit 16-2

PERSONALITY SCORING SHEET

STRENGTHS

	Sanguine	Choleric	Melancholy	Phlegmatic
1	Adventurous	Adaptable	Animated	Analytical
2	Persistent	Playful	Persuasive	Peaceful
3	Submissive	Self-sacrificing	Sociable	Strong-willed
4	Considerate	Controlled	Competitive	Convincing
5	Refreshing	Respectful	Reserved	Resourceful
6	Satisfied	Sensitive	Self-reliant	Spirited
7	Planner	Patient	Positive	Promoter
8	Sure	Spontaneous	Scheduled	Shy
9	Orderly	Obliging	Outspoken	Optimistic
10	Friendly	Faithful	Funny	Forceful
11	Daring	Delightful	Diplomatic	Detailed
12	Cheerful	Consistent	Cultured	Confident
13	Idealistic	Independent	Inoffensive	Inspiring
14	Demonstrative	Decisive	Dry humor	Deep
15	Mediator	Musical	Mover	Mixes Easily
16	Thoughtful	Tenacious	Talker	Tolerant
17	Listener	Loyal	Leader	Lively
18	Contented	Chief	Chartmaker	Cute
19	Perfectionist	Permissive	Productive	Popular
20	Bouncy	Bold	Behaved	Balanced

TOTALS

Exhibit 16-2

WEAKNESSES

	Sanguine	Choleric	Melancholy	Phlegmatic
21	Blank	Bashful	Brassy	Bossy
22	Undisciplined	Unsympathetic	Unenthusiastic	Unforgiving
23	Reticent	Resentful	Resistant	Repetitious
24	Fussy	Fearful	Forgetful	Frank
25	Impatient	Insecure	Indecisive	Interrupts
26	Unpopular	Uninvolved	Unpredictable	Unaffectionate
27	Headstrong	Haphazard	Hard to please	Hesitant
28	Plain	Pessimistic	Proud	Permissive
29	Angered easily	Aimless	Argumentative	Alienated
30	Naive	Negative attitude	Nervy	Nonchalant
31	Worrier	Withdrawn	Workaholic	Wants credit
32	Too sensitive	Tactless	Timid	Talkative
33	Doubtful	Disorganized	Domineering	Depressed
34	Inconsistent	Introvert	Intolerant	Indifferent
35	Messy	Moody	Mumbles	Manipulative
36	Slow	Stubborn	Show-off	Skeptical
37	Loner	Lord over	Lazy	Loud
38	Sluggish	Suspicious	Short-tempered	Scatterbrained
39	Revengeful	Restless	Reluctant	Rash
40	Compromising	Critical	Crafty	Changeable
TOTALS				
COMBINED TOTALS				

Exhibit 16-2

STRENGTHS

EMOTIONS

Sanguine	Choleric	Melancholy	Phlegmatic
Appealing personality	Born leader	Deep and thoughtful	Low-key personality
Talkative, storyteller	Dynamic and active	Analytical	Easygoing and relaxed
Life of the party	Compulsive need for change	Serious and purposeful	Calm, cool, and collected
Good sense of humor	Must correct wrongs	Genius prone	Patient, well balanced
Memory for color	Strong-willed and decisive	Talented and creative	Consistent life
Physically holds on to listener	Unemotional	Artistic or musical	Quiet, but witty
Emotional and demonstrative	Not easily discouraged	Philosophical and poetic	Sympathetic and kind
Enthusiastic and expressive	Independent and self-sufficient	Appreciative of beauty	Keeps emotions hidden
Cheerful and bubbling over	Exudes confidence	Sensitive to others	Happily reconciled to life
Curious	Can run anything	Self-sacrificing	All-purpose person
Wide-eyed and innocent		Conscientious	
Lives in the present		Idealistic	
Changeable disposition			
Sincere at heart			
Always a child			

WORK

Sanguine	Choleric	Melancholy	Phlegmatic
Volunteers for jobs	Goal oriented	Schedule oriented	Competent and steady
Thinks up new activities	Sees the whole picture	Perfectionist, high standards	Peaceful and agreeable
Looks great on the surface	Organizes well	Detail conscious	Has administrative ability
Creative and colorful	Seeks practical solutions	Persistent and thorough	Mediates problems
Has energy and enthusiasm	Moves quickly to action	Orderly and organized	Avoids conflicts
Starts in a flashy way	Delegates work	Neat and tidy	Good under pressure
Inspires others to join	Insists on production	Economical	Finds the easy way
Charms others to work	Makes the goal	Sees the problems	
	Stimulates activity	Finds creative solutions	
	Thrives on opposition	Needs to finish what he starts	
		Likes charts, graphs, figures, lists	

FRIENDS

Sanguine	Choleric	Melancholy	Phlegmatic
Makes friends easily	Has little need for friends	Makes friends cautiously	Easy to get along with
Loves people	Will work for group activity	Content to stay in background	Pleasant and enjoyable
Thrives on compliments	Will lead and organize	Avoids causing attention	Inoffensive
Seems exciting	Is usually right	Faithful and devoted	Good listener
Envied by others	Excels in emergencies	Will listen to complaints	Dry sense of humor
Doesn't hold grudges		Can solve other's problems	Enjoys watching people
Apologizes quickly		Deep concern for other people	Has many friends
Presents dull moments		Moved to tears with compassion	Has compassion and concern
Likes spontaneous activities		Seeks ideal mate	

Exhibit 16-2

WEAKNESSES

	Sanguine	Choleric	Melancholy	Phlegmatic
EMOTIONS	Compulsive talker	Bossy	Remembers the negatives	Unenthusiastic
	Exaggerates and elaborates	Impatient	Moody and depressed	Fearful and worried
	Dwells on trivia	Quick-tempered	Enjoys being hurt	Indecisive
	Can't remember names	Can't relax	Has false humility	Avoids responsibility
	Scares others off	Too impetuous	Off in another world	Quiet will of iron
	Too happy for some	Enjoys controversy and arguments	Low self-image	Selfish
	Has restless energy	Won't give up when losing	Has selective hearing	Too shy and reticent
	Egotistical	Comes on too strong	Self-centered	Too compromising
	Blusters and complains	Inflexible	Too introspective	Self-righteous
	Naive, gets taken in	Is not complimentary	Guilt feelings	
	Has loud voice and laugh	Dislikes tears and emotions	Persecution complex	
	Controlled by circumstances	Is unsympathetic	Tends to hypochondria	
	Gets angry easily			
	Seems phony to some			
	Never grows up			
WORK	Would rather talk	Little tolerance for mistakes	Not people oriented	Not goal oriented
	Forgets obligations	Doesn't analyze details	Depressed over imperfections	Lacks self-motivation
	Doesn't follow through	Bored by trivia	Chooses difficult work	Hard to get moving
	Confidence fades fast	May make rash decisions	Hesitant to start projects	Resents being pushed
	Undisciplined	May be rude or tactless	Spends too much time planning	Lazy and careless
	Priorities out of order	Manipulates people	Prefers analysis to work	Discourages others
	Decides by feelings	Demanding of others	Self-deprecating	Would rather watch
	Easily distracted	End justifies the means	Hard to please	
	Wastes time talking	Work my become his god	Standards often too high	
		Demands loyalty in the ranks	Deep need for approval	
FRIENDS	Hates to be alone	Tends to use people	Lives through others	Dampens enthusiasm
	Needs to be center stage	Dominates others	Insecure socially	Stays uninvolved
	Wants to be popular	Decides for others	Withdrawn and remote	Is not exciting
	Looks for credit	Knows everything	Critical of others	Indifferent to plans
	Dominates conversations	Can do everything better	Holds back affection	Judges others
	Interrupts and doesn't listen	Is too independent	Dislikes those in opposition	Sarcastic and teasing
	Answers for others	Possessive of friends and mate	Suspicious of people	Resists change
	Fickle and forgetful	Can't say, "I'm sorry"	Antagonistic and vengeful	
	Makes excuses	May be right, but unpopular	Unforgiving	
	Repeats stories		Full of contradictions	
			Skeptical of compliments	

Reprinted from AFTER EVERY WEDDING COMES A MARRIAGE, Florence Littauer, Harvest House Publishers

Exhibit 16-3

MOTIVATIONAL NEEDS SURVEY

1. Describe a recent job situation in which you experienced a sense of satisfaction and fulfillment.

   _____

   _____

   _____

   Identify the closest match of your situation to the choices listed below:

   ❑ a. A specific goal was accomplished
   ❑ b. Warm, fulfilling relationships were established
   ❑ c. A group of people were influenced

2. If you could choose between three work-related projects in which to participate over the next several months, select the one you would enjoy the most:

   ❑ a. A project in which you have responsibility for finding the solution to a chronic problem in your organization
   ❑ b. A project requiring a cooperative effort with your peer group
   ❑ c. A project requiring you to direct and control the efforts of a group of people

3. In your day-to-day job situation, which option provides you the greatest sense of satisfaction?

   ❑ a. Taking a calculated risk and seeing it pay off
   ❑ b. Being accepted and liked by a group
   ❑ c. Giving direction and supervision

Exhibit 16-3

4. On a weekly basis, what do you look forward to doing the most?

    ❑ a. Finding solutions to problems which prevent goals from being reached

    ❑ b. Promoting harmonious working relationships among those in your work group

    ❑ c. Using persuasive skills to influence the work of others

5. Your closest associate or friend would describe you as a person who:

    ❑ a. Looks for greater challenges

    ❑ b. Makes friends and acquaintances easily

    ❑ c. Likes to participate in a good argument

6. What would be the most important factor in helping you accomplish your job?

    ❑ a. Concrete feedback on how you are doing

    ❑ b. An opportunity to interact with others

    ❑ c. The amount of authority you can exercise

7. Describe the ingredients you would build into your *ideal* job assignment.

_____

_____

_____

Select the closest match of the *most important* ingredient with the following choices:

Exhibit 16-3

☐ a. Offers an opportunity to accomplish something significant

☐ b. Provides an opportunity to work as part of a team

☐ c. Offers you an opportunity to significantly influence the efforts of others

8. At the end of a project, what type of reward would you prefer?

☐ a. Personal satisfaction in knowing that a goal has been reached

☐ b. Respect and admiration from your work group

☐ c. Recognition and advancement through the formal organization

9. When you daydream what do you tend to think about?

☐ a. Accomplishing new and challenging goals

☐ b. Warm, friendly relationships within the organization

☐ c. Rising to the top of the organization

10. In a group situation which would you prefer?

☐ a. To make the greatest contribution of the group

☐ b. To be the best liked person in the group

☐ c. To be the leader of the group

Exhibit 16-3

MOTIVATIONAL NEEDS PROFILE

Score	A	B	C
10	_____	_____	_____
9	_____	_____	_____
8	_____	_____	_____
7	_____	_____	_____
6	_____	_____	_____
5	_____	_____	_____
4	_____	_____	_____
3	_____	_____	_____
2	_____	_____	_____
1	_____	_____	_____
0	_____	_____	_____

Exhibit 16-3

MOTIVATIONAL NEEDS DESCRIPTION

Achievement Motivation

1. Tends to spend time thinking of goals and how they can be attained
2. Has an attraction for finding solutions to problems
3. Enjoys taking calculated risks
4. Seeks specific and concrete feedback on the quality of his work
5. Eagerly accepts more responsibility and challenging tasks

Affiliation Motivation

1. Tends to spend time thinking of warm, fulfilling relationships
2. Promotes harmonious situations vs. Conflict within relationships
3. Finds or desires satisfaction from being liked and accepted in the group
4. Seeks situations which require working in cooperation with others
5. Tends to make friends easily

Influence Motivation

1. Tends to spend time thinking of how to influence others or how to control the means of influencing others
2. Seeks positions of leadership in social or work groups
3. Desires to give direction vs. taking orders
4. Tends to be verbally expressive and enjoys a good argument
5. Seeks high status positions or positions requiring persuasive skills

Exhibit 16-4

My Covenant

I commit myself this day to become an effective disciple of Jesus Christ. I will give myself to reaching my full potential, and becoming all that God wants me to be.

In order to reach this goal, I understand that God must prepare me in some specific areas. My character must be polished. My gifts must be developed. My passion must be focused. My attitudes and lifestyle must be groomed.

Desiring to cooperate in obedience, I agree to participate in a mentoring experience, meeting with my partner as scheduled on a regular basis. I recognize that my mentor is only a tool in God's hands. I plan, however, to follow through on all lessons and assignments in cooperation with God's purposes to build me into a disciple He can trust. I plan to submit to the accountability of my mentor and/or partner. I purpose to finish well, regardless of my human tendency to seek shortcuts or simply quit. I resolve to find my own person to mentor once we've completed this commitment.

Before God, I sign this covenant, and purpose to allow Him to use this experience to make me the person He wants me to be.

*Signed:*_____ *Date:*_____
      Mentee

*Signed:*_____ *Date:*_____
      Mentor

Exhibit 16-5

MENTORING COVENANT GUIDELINES

Your covenant is an agreement to work toward common stated goals. Prayerfully use this tool to stimulate yourselves to press on toward the goal of Christlikeness.

1. Be sure to exchange all necessary information for contact and communication. (Phone numbers, address, fax numbers, e-mail address, etc.)

2. Define your purpose and goals. List 3-5 goals you plan to accomplish. Be sure to clarify your expectations for this mentoring relationship. Unmet expectations are deadly to the health and growth of a mentoring relationship and ministry.

   Discuss the Mentor's areas of strengths such as modeling prayer, evangelism, decision making, parenting, organization, priority setting, time management, etc. Discuss the Mentee's areas of need and expectations.

In their book, *Connecting*, Paul Stanley and Robert Clinton outline seven different kinds of mentoring roles.

1. **Discipler:** Helping with the basics of following Christ.
2. **Spiritual Guide:** Accountability; direction/insight for maturation.
3. **Coach:** Motivation; skills needed to meet a task or challenge.
4. **Counselor:** Timely advice; perspective on self, others, ministry.
5. **Teacher:** Knowledge and understanding of a specific subject.

Exhibit 16-5

6. **Sponsor:** Career guidance; protection; relational networking.

7. **Model:** Personal model or example for life, ministry or career.

Use this guide to help determine the kind of mentoring that will take place.

3. Determine when and how often you will meet.

4. Agree together how you will hold each other accountable and responsible. This is a crucial step for the health and success of your mentoring relationship.

5. Confidentiality represents a sacred trust between two parties. Discuss this component with understanding and ultimate agreement.

6. The length and life cycle of a mentoring relationship will vary to some degree. Realize the need to set a reasonable length of time to be involved. *Avoid open-ended relationships.* Build in periodic times for evaluation. Focus on a one-year commitment.

7. "Begin with the end in mind." Strive to have a healthy closing to the official relationship. Celebrate what God has done and make plans to find another "faithful [person] who will teach [mentor] others also."

What To Do In A Mentoring Meeting

It is in this final chapter that we get down to the brass tacks. We will discuss the goal of the mentor and exactly what we should do in the meeting with our mentees. I'll do my best to give you the big picture and the feel of a typical meeting. I want to speak in an especially practical and personal fashion with you in this final section. I dedicate this chapter to the purpose of enabling you to get the very most out of your mentoring experience.

SETTING UP THE MEETING

Stu Weber, author of *Locking Arms*, writes about "the buddy system." He remembers his days in elementary school, as well as his days in the military, where he learned to use and appreciate the buddy system. This is simply a system of support and accountability where everyone in the group finds a partner—and sticks with them. When his army sergeant told the troop to find a buddy, he remembers that he and most of the other guys in formation would have preferred jumping off a cliff, doing fifty push-ups or running ten miles in full battle gear. Later, however, he saw that the buddy system probably saved a number of kids' lives in school and a large volume of soldiers in Vietnam.

The point is that all of us need to find a "buddy" and take initiative to stick with them! I have found that the mentor in a relationship usually has to give permission to the mentee to set up their meetings together. Hence, in the beginning, the mentor must take initiative. After a few weeks, however, the mentee ought to exhibit enough spiritual hunger to pursue his mentor and take initiative to set up the meetings. Both will have to determine the frequency.

The meetings you have with your mentee should be held in a comfortable and safe setting. By safe, I mean an atmosphere where honest, transparent discussion can occur. As you ask each other personal questions, you will want to envision how safe you both will feel about conversing out loud about certain issues in public places. Accountability is best implemented in private.

If you are conversing over a "principle" and an assignment, I would suggest you begin by discussing the truth principle first, then its application. If the assignment is one that the two of you can do together—by all means do so. This may require your scheduled meeting that week to be out on a university campus where you'll be sharing your faith together, or in a solitary place where you can pray at length together. The goal is simply that you think through the best possible place to dialogue and to accomplish life change.

THE MEETING

Once you sit down to meet, take initiative to set the tone and atmoshpere. Ask about their week and take a few moments to review their personal life. Don't just jump into the "business." If you're prone to skip to the "business" just remember that their life *is* the business, and the reason why you meet.

I've found it wise to begin the process with an initial meeting or two to clarify expectations on both sides. I ask them to list three goals or expectations that they would like to get out of the experience. Then I verbalize three of my own expectations or goals for them. I also attempt to convey the depth of my commitment to them. I cast vision for the potential I see in them and where they could go—if they want to. All of this lays a solid foundation for your subsequent meetings.

ASKING THE RIGHT QUESTIONS

As you think through the big picture of your discussion together, perhaps the little acrostic of SALT will help you follow an appropriate flow of dialogue:

S - SAY SOMETHING AFFIRMING

A - ASK THE RIGHT QUESTIONS

L - LISTEN WELL

T - TURN THE DISCUSSION TO THE TRUTH (PRINCIPLE) TO BE LEARNED

As you ask the questions, keep in mind that this may be your primary role in the meeting. The student may simply need you to probe like a doctor examining a patient. Doctors are always good at poking and prodding their patients during a physical examination to see "where it hurts."

INDUCTIVE APPROACH

This probing and prodding is another way of describing the *inductive approach* to the art of mentoring. In the same way that effective evangelism is best accomplished through probing inductively to see where the perceived need is on the part of the non-Christian, so it is true with mentoring. We should not approach our mentee with a package that we plan to jam down their throat whether they like it or not. That is the deductive approach. Instead, we must observe and diagnose what the issues are, then begin to address them. Again, this will require you to master the art of asking questions.

That's what you must become proficient at doing. Your questions may flow best in this order:

♦ HIGHLIGHTS:
- What were the highlights of the lesson/assignment for you?
- What stood out in your mind, or made the biggest impact?
- What was the number one truth you learned from this lesson/assignment?

♦ STRUGGLES:
- What were the chief struggles you had with the topic?
- Did you have any internal battles with the assignment?
- Do you have any barriers in your life that keep you from obedience?

♦ OPPORTUNITIES:
- What will it take to master this Kingdom issue?
- How will you attempt to obey God in this area? (What new ways?)
- How can you further network with people/books to see life change in this area?
- In what ways could God's Kingdom advance if you practice this truth?

Asking these questions will end up being more profound than an eloquent lecture from you. The reason is simply this: asking questions encourages *them* to come up with and *own* the answers, not you. As you learn to "host" the conversation, you can guide them toward a biblical response without just giving it to them.

Glen Urquhart and Bobb Biehl suggest some additions to this format when you want to simply discuss their personal goals. The mentee (or protege) should come to the meeting prepared to discuss:

A. A list of 1-3 upcoming DECISIONS to which the mentor can give perspective.

B. A list of 1-3 PROBLEMS in reaching the protege's goals to discuss with the mentor for perspective and help.

C. A list of PLANS for the mentor's general information and update.

D. A list of PROGRESS POINTS so the mentor is updated and can give well-deserved praise.

E. A list of PRAYER REQUESTS for the mentor's prayers and general support.

F. Personal roadblocks, blind spots, and fears the protege would like to discuss.

DRAWING THE RIGHT CONCLUSIONS

Once they have distilled the proper conclusion or personal response, you will likely be the one to hold them accountable to make application. I always try to have a pen ready, and as they draw conclusions, I jot them down on a pad of paper and keep them in a folder under their name. Then I would begin this series of questions. . .

- ◆   Do you really believe and embrace that truth?
- ◆   How can I best hold you accountable to practice it?
- ◆   What could be your first step?
- ◆   When could you take it?

The point is not to press them into some performance trap, but rather to take them past mere intellectual assent into willful obedience (James 2:26). These lessons *must* go beyond mental gymnastics. And for most of us, that only happens when we are held accountable. Decide now to hold your mentee accountable in their obedience.

SETTING A GOAL FOR YOUR MENTORING

Obviously, it would be ridiculous to mentor someone without possessing a goal. We should always have the end result in mind when we meet with our mentee.

So what is the goal of our mentoring? What do we want our mentees to look like as the result of our investment in their lives? Good questions. These are the kinds of things you and your mentee ought to jot down in one of your earlier meetings. If you are mentoring someone in a business setting, you will set business related goals. If you are ministering in a church context, you may set ministry related goals. Context has a lot to do with both your goals and authority as a mentor.

Spiritually speaking, let me suggest a biblical goal for you and your mentee to pursue. Since Jesus Christ had but one significant prayer request in His three-and-a-half year ministry, it might be good to examine that request and pursue it as a goal. The passage goes like this:

"The harvest is plentiful but the laborers are few.

Pray, therefore, to the Lord of the harvest to send out *laborers* into His harvest." (Matthew 9:36-38)

Jesus prayed for laborers. In fact, I believe the number one goal of His mentoring of the twelve was to turn laypeople into laborers. My definition of a laborer is threefold:

1) An intimate disciple of Jesus Christ,

2) Who uses their gifts to advance God's Kingdom, and

3) Who is committed to reproducing other laborers.

If you work toward this end, you will have made a significant contribution to God's Kingdom in that person's life. Anything else you end up with will be icing on the cake. Your goal should include all three facets of the above definition and should never fall short of spiritual reproduction. Your mentee should eventually be able to mentor someone else.

HOSTING THE DISCUSSION...

One final reminder. Nearly every relationship and every conversation has both a host and a guest. I have drawn this conclusion after years of observation. People seem to find their place in discussions as either the proactive guide (the host) or the responder (the guest).

These terms, "host" and "guest," are most often used in the context of a visitor to a home or party. A good host, upon opening the door and seeing the guest who's just arrived, will generally take charge and do certain things. They first say something like, "Won't you come in?" Later they'll say, "May I take your coat?" and "Have a seat" and "Would you like something to drink?"

Each of these illustrates that the host is assuming the proper place of leadership, even if the topic of conversation is the choice of the guest. We all know how to be a good host without ever needing to read a book on it. The host is the relational leader by the mere fact that the context is on his or her home turf.

Within the mentoring relationship, I am challenging you, the mentor, to host the relationship. This does not mean you have to have the gift of gab or have something witty or profound to say on every subject. It simply means that you are the *guide*, making sure that the two of you get to your destination.

As the mentee calls you to set up the appointment, be as gracious as you can be. Welcome them into your life each and every time you make contact. As you invite them in, have questions ready, just as we discussed earlier. In fact, let me encourage you to enter each meeting armed with this arsenal:

- Have four or five questions ready.
- Set your demeanor to be safe and affirming.
- Decide that *you* will lead the way in being open and vulnerable.
- Maintain a sense of the big picture—where is God leading this subject?
- Be ready to speak into their life concerning process items they must face.

Review the principles in Chapter 8 of this handbook, "How Do I Speak With Authority into Someone's Life?" In that section I review how to gain influence in the life of a student. My acrostic, again, is simply:

HOW TO GAIN INFLUENCE WITH PEOPLE

I - INVESTMENT IN PEOPLE
N - NATURAL WITH PEOPLE
F - FAITH IN PEOPLE
L - LISTENING TO PEOPLE
U - UNDERSTANDING OF PEOPLE
E - ENCOURAGER TO PEOPLE
N - NAVIGATE FOR PEOPLE
C - CONCERN FOR PEOPLE
E - ENTHUSIASM OVER PEOPLE

It is my consistent prayer that you demonstrate these functions with your mentee. You are embarking on one of the most strategic endeavors of your spiritual life. You are now entering a ministry of multiplication!

In early 1996, my wife and I went to see a movie that has become indelibly etched into my mind. It was the highly acclaimed film, *Mr. Holland's Opus.* Richard Dreyfus plays the part of a musician whose goal was to write and perform music, and become famous. He was very honest about this personal goal, and he and his wife endeavored to do whatever it took to reach it.

He decided to take a teaching job at a local high school to save enough money to make it big in music. Somewhere en route, however, his goals and values changed. I write about this change in my devotional guide, *The Greatest Mentors in the Bible.* He stays at the teaching position for thirty years. At some point during all the classroom hours, he began to go beyond being merely a teacher—and became a mentor. He began to invest in the students, as persons, after class. He began to make one to one deposits in their hearts. By the end of the film he has impacted literally hundreds of students. Their lives have been changed because he got involved in relationships—and they returned to their alma mater years later to say "thanks" to their mentor.

I love this story because it reminds me of my own life. Mr. Holland is a picture of a reluctant mentor. He didn't want to get involved in the messes of human need. He just wanted to teach class between 9:00 a.m. and 4:00 p.m. and then go home. But his conscience wouldn't let him. He had to begin to coach these kids through life decisions. Because of that commitment, he made his contribution to changing the lives of countless young people.

May others be able to say the same things about our lives when we're through. I pray God's blessings on you as you bless others!

Praying For A Mentee

Pray and ask God to make clear who He wants to be your mentors and your mentees. Remember the warning of Psalm 1:

"Blessed is the man who walketh *NOT* in the counsel of the ungodly. . . ." Pray to have a godly mentor as the Psalm infers.

If you could have any Mentor(s) in the world. . .which person would you ask first, second, and third?

1. _____

2. _____

3. _____

Note: You may have three or more mentors at a time, each helping you win in different areas of your life (i.e., one spiritual mentor, one professional mentor, and one social mentor).

What three young people do you feel have the very highest potential for leadership/ministry...who may be open to your mentoring today?

1. _____

2. _____

3. _____

Start with one to three mentees first.

Start with one or, at the most, three mentees. When they grow to the point where they require less of your time and become capable of mentoring, you can begin mentoring others and so can they!

I believe the effort you put forth in mentoring others will be the best investment you will ever make!

NOTES. . .

_____

_____

_____

_____

_____

_____

_____

_____

_____

_____

_____

NOTES. . .